PENGUIN PASSNOTES

Silas Marner

Susan Quilliam was born in Liverpool and educated at Liverpool University. After a period of teaching she moved to London where she works in publishing and as a freelance writer. She has also written the study guide to *Pride and Prejudice*, *A Man for All Seasons*, *Kes*, *Romeo and Juliet* and *My Family and Other Animals* in the Penguin Passnote Series, and is preparing future volumes, including *A Taste of Honey*.

PENGUIN PASSNOTES

GEORGE ELIOT

Silas Marner

S. QUILLIAM

ADVISORY EDITOR: S. H. COOTE M.A., PH.D.

PENGUIN BOOKS

Penguin Books Ltd, Harmondsworth, Middlesex, England
Viking Penguin Inc., 40 West 23rd Street, New York, New York 10010, U.S.A.
Penguin Books Australia Ltd, Ringwood, Victoria, Australia
Penguin Books Canada Limited, 2801 John Street, Markham, Ontario, Canada L3R 1B4
Penguin Books (N.Z.) Ltd, 182–190 Wairau Road, Auckland 10, New Zealand

First published 1984
Reprinted 1986

Made and printed in Great Britain by
Richard Clay (The Chaucer Press) Ltd, Bungay, Suffolk
Set in Monophoto Ehrhardt

The publishers are grateful to the following Examination Boards for permission to reproduce questions from examination papers used in individual titles in the Passnotes series:

Associated Examining Board, University of Cambridge Local Examinations Syndicate, Joint Matriculation Board, University of London School Examinations Department, Oxford and Cambridge Schools Examination Board, University of Oxford Delegacy of Local Examinations.

Contents

To the Student

This book is designed to help you with your O-level or C.S.E. English Literature examination. It contains a synopsis of the plot, a glossary of the more unfamiliar words and phrases, and a commentary on some of the issues raised by the text. An account of the writer's life is also included for background.

Page references in parentheses are to the Penguin Classics edition, edited by Q. D. Leavis.

When you use this book remember that it is no more than an aid to your study. It will help you find passages quickly and perhaps give you some ideas for essays. But remember: *This book is not a substitute for reading the text and it is your knowledge and your response that matter*. These are the things the examiners are looking for, and they are also the things that will give you the most pleasure. Show your knowledge and appreciation to the examiner, and show them clearly.

Introduction

THE LIFE AND BACKGROUND OF GEORGE ELIOT (1819–80)

George Eliot was the pen-name of Mary Ann Evans. She was born in 1819 in Warwickshire, which was then a region of small villages very much like the Raveloe of *Silas Marner*. George Eliot loved the countryside, and she grew to know it well. When she was five, however, she went to school in Nuneaton, where she received a good education and was found to be intelligent and talented.

While at school, she became friends with one of the teachers, Maria Lewis. Maria's Evangelicalism influenced her to such an extent that she became a convert at the age of fifteen. As we will see in our section on religion (pp. 66–70), Evangelical belief was both fervent and strict; George Eliot remained deeply committed to it until she was in her early twenties.

When she had completed her education George Eliot returned home. Her mother had died when she was sixteen, so she kept house for her father. Gradually, all the Evans children married except herself, and the future may have seemed bleak to her, with nothing to look forward to except loneliness and looking after her father. But she did have a number of friends, and she spent much of her time studying and reading.

In 1841 she and her father moved to Coventry and she started work as a translator. At the same time, she began to have doubts about her own beliefs, about organized religion as a whole, and even about the existence of God. She stopped going to church for a time, but the family reaction was so disapproving that she resumed attendance. George Eliot never surrendered her belief in the paramount importance in our lives of a love of humanity, but from then on she strongly questioned the practices of formal Christianity. We can see this in her comments in *Silas Marner* on Lantern Yard and the Raveloe church. Her beliefs about the superior value of loving kindness in human relationships are, of course, of the greatest significance in the book.

While rethinking her religious views, George Eliot was also developing her professional life. She published translations and began work as assistant editor on the *Westminster Review*, an important philosophical journal. This meant that she mixed with many of the leading radical thinkers of the day. When her father died in 1849, the resulting freedom allowed her to become deeply involved in London's intellectual circles.

In 1854 George Eliot met the man who was to be her friend and companion for the next twenty-four years. George Henry Lewes was an unconventional man, a thinker and writer whose ideas on free love had encouraged both him and his wife to have relationships outside their marriage. Because of this it was impossible for Lewes to get a divorce, so George Eliot bravely agreed to live with him while he was still married. For a considerable time she was ostracized by London society for making this decision, and her family did not accept her back until after Lewes's death.

Now settled with a man she loved, George Eliot continued with her work and was encouraged by Lewes to write fiction as well as the translations and criticism on which she had so far been engaged. She began with *Scenes of Clerical Life* (1857), which was an immediate success. Because she was a woman and was living in an unacceptable situation, however, she continued to use her adopted pen-name. She followed her first novel with *Adam Bede* (1859), *The Mill on the Floss* (1860) and *Silas Marner* (1861).

The story of how *Silas Marner* came to be written is an interesting one. George Eliot had moved to a particularly depressing house in London, and in her new home she must have felt as out of place and unhappy as Silas does in Raveloe. She was working on her novel

Romola when an idea suddenly came to her. She remembered having seen, when she was a child, 'a linen weaver with a bag on his back' who seemed to be an outcast; from this single image grew *Silas Marner*. She wrote the book immediately, leaving off work on *Romola* to do so. For a while she thought of dealing with the weaver's story in verse, but then realized that prose would give her greater scope for humour and developed characterization.

The original vision, as we see from the finished novel, evolved into a work about many of the ideas that concerned George Eliot. In her native Warwickshire she had witnessed the Industrial Revolution and its attendant problems. She had experienced at first hand the struggle to find a place in one's life for religion and loving kindness. Country life and the difficulties of adapting to a foreign environment were also subjects dear to her heart. Her childhood had led her to love the countryside, and she was much influenced by the literary movement called Romanticism, which laid great stress on the importance of both natural, rural surroundings and natural human relationships. Its leading poet, Wordsworth, was George Eliot's own favourite, and *Silas Marner* begins with lines from one of his works. All in all, therefore, the book reflects not only the author's ideas but a great deal that is relevant to her own life.

After finishing *Silas Marner*, which was an instant success, in 1861, George Eliot completed *Romola* (1862–3). She continued to work, writing *Felix Holt* (1866), *Middlemarch* (1871–2) and *Daniel Deronda* (1874–6), as well as some verse drama, poetry and essays. Within her own lifetime she was considered a great writer, as well as a popular one.

In 1878 Lewes died. Shortly after this, in May 1880, George Eliot married a close friend, J. W. Cross. It seems likely that she valued his companionship; certainly the marriage led to society's renewed acceptance of her, and even to her family's forgiveness. George Eliot died in December 1880, and was buried in Westminster Abbey.

It may be difficult for us to see *Silas Marner*, a tale of nineteenth-century country life, as relevant to our own twentieth-century lives. In fact, although the environment may be very different, the problems are the same. The challenges of industrialization, of being uprooted from one's original surroundings, and of living at peace with other people and oneself; these are all topics we read about every day, and which we often have to cope with ourselves. George Eliot wrote about problems that were relevant to her and her society, but we can still appreciate these problems and learn from the solutions she offers.

Synopsis of Silas Marner

Silas Marner is the tale of a linen weaver living in the country village of Raveloe in the early years of the nineteenth century. The villagers regard him with suspicion because he is an outsider from the urban region of North'ard (p. 54). They also think him strange because he has fits during which he seems to fall into unconsciousness.

In fact, Silas Marner left North'ard after being falsely accused of theft by the congregation of the chapel to which he belonged (pp. 56–62). This incident, particularly since it was instigated by his best friend, William Dane, has made Silas lose all faith in God and humanity. He moves to the countryside, a completely alien place, and buries himself in his work, cut off from other people and interested only in the gold he earns (pp. 62–70). He becomes a miser.

It is the winter of Silas's fifteenth year in Raveloe. The most affluent people in the village are the Cass family. Godfrey, the eldest son, has fallen into a secret and unhappy marriage with Molly Farren, a barmaid (p. 75). He really wants to marry Nancy Lammeter, the daughter of another respected Raveloe family. Dunsey Cass, who is blackmailing his brother by threatening to reveal everything, takes Godfrey's horse to the hunt, arranging to sell it and pocket the money to pay his debts. The horse is killed while hunting (pp. 82–5), and Dunsey has to walk home, nearly penniless. On the way, he passes Silas Marner's cottage near the Stone-pits (p. 87) and, remembering the gossip about the miser's money, calls at the house to try to tempt the gold from him (p. 88). The cottage is empty. Dunsey quickly realizes where the money is hidden (p. 89), takes it, and slips away unnoticed (p. 90).

Returning home, Silas Marner discovers the gold is missing and becomes desperate (pp. 90–95). He rushes off to the local inn, the

Rainbow, where the country folk, who have been deep in discussion and reminiscence (pp. 95–105), realize he is in genuine trouble and help him (pp. 106–11). An investigation is begun. No thief is found, but everyone suspects an unknown travelling pedlar (pp. 111--15). The gold seems gone for ever. No one suspects that Dunsey is responsible.

Realizing how upset Silas is, the villagers rally round (pp. 130–33), particularly kind Dolly Winthrop. She brings Silas food (p. 134) and tries to persuade him to attend church (pp. 136–9), which he has not done since his unjust accusation at North'ard. The weaver is so little used to meeting people, however, that he cannot respond to the villagers' kindness (p. 140), and even spends Christmas alone without visiting neighbours or going to church (p. 140).

In the meantime, Dunsey has not returned home. We learn later that, after leaving Silas's cottage, he had fallen into the Stone-pits and been drowned. No one is particularly concerned. Godfrey, hearing the story of the dead horse from one of Dunsey's friends (pp. 115–18), realizes that he will have to tell his father at least part of the truth (pp. 118–20). But he cannot bring himself to confess the exact hold Dunsey has over him (pp. 120–23). Squire Cass, having expressed his anger over the dead horse, lets the matter rest. At the same time he encourages Godfrey to propose to Nancy, and cannot understand why he is unwilling to do so; especially as the ideal opportunity, the New Year's Eve ball, is very near (pp. 123–6).

On New Year's Eve, the neighbouring families gather at the Casses' house (pp. 143–60). Godfrey, feeling more confident because Dunsey has not come back, begins to court Nancy again (pp. 155–63). In fact, Godfrey's wife Molly is at that very moment on her way to see him, carrying his child and intending to shame him into acknowledging their marriage (pp. 163–4). But in her drugged state she falls asleep in the snow, and her baby wanders off into Silas Marner's cottage (pp. 165–6). The weaver is standing at the door, unaware of what is happening because of one of his fits (pp. 166–7). When he wakes, Silas sees the gleam of the baby's hair and thinks his gold has been returned (pp. 167–8).

When he discovers the truth, and finds the baby's mother dead in the snow outside (p. 169), Silas goes for help to Squire Cass's house (p. 171). Help is sent, and the village women offer to take care of the baby. Silas, however, refuses to part with her (p. 172).

Godfrey sees the baby and understands what must have happened. When the unknown woman's death is confirmed, he feels thoroughly relieved, and convinces himself that the best thing now is to hide the truth (pp. 171-7). The baby is cared for by Silas, and Godfrey is able to concentrate on winning Nancy for his wife and beginning his own family. He eases his conscience by occasionally helping Silas with money and goods, as do many of the villagers (pp. 178–92).

The child, whom Silas names Eppie, changes the weaver's life. Because she is growing up and enjoying the world, nature and other people, Silas starts to respond to these things, too; as the baby develops, so does the weaver. He is accepted more and more by village society because of her, and, helped by Dolly (pp. 178–91), he begins to regain his faith in God.

Sixteen years later, we see the Raveloe community leaving church one autumn Sunday morning (p. 195). Godfrey and Nancy are older but only slightly altered.

Silas looks aged and weak, but Eppie is now a beautiful eighteen-year-old. Her affection makes Silas's life worth living. She helps him perceive the good in the world (p. 205). She is also admired by Dolly Winthrop's son, Aaron (pp. 196–9). After Sunday lunch (p. 200) Silas and Eppie go outside, where they notice that Godfrey Cass has begun to have the Stone-pits drained so as to begin dairy-farming on nearby land (p. 207). After a while Eppie mentions that Aaron has suggested marriage to her. Silas realizes that he is getting older and will soon be unable to support Eppie, so, although neither wants change, they consider the idea (pp. 208–10).

At the Casses' house, Nancy spends Sunday afternoon thinking over the past years (pp. 214–20). Her one disappointment is that her child died (p. 215) and that the childless marriage upsets Godfrey. He has suggested adopting Eppie (pp. 216–17), but Nancy, still unaware that the girl is Godfrey's child, sees this as defying Providence (pp. 216–20). Godfrey soon comes in, deeply shocked (p. 221). Dunsey's body has been discovered while the Stone-pits were being drained, and with the body was found Silas's gold, obviously stolen by Dunsey (p. 222). Godfrey, realizing that truth will always come to light, confesses his previous marriage to Molly (p. 223). To his surprise, Nancy forgives him and, knowing now that Eppie is Godfrey's child, fully agrees with his plan to adopt her (pp. 224–5).

Nancy and Godfrey visit Silas's cottage (p. 227) and suggest that they should take care of Eppie. She, however, says she will not leave the weaver (p. 230). Godfrey, desperate now to have his child back, tells Eppie that he is her real father and challenges Silas to stand in her way (pp. 230–32). Because of his love for Eppie, Silas wants her to have the best in life; but Eppie's love for her foster father makes her unwavering in her decision to stay (pp. 233–4). The Casses leave, eventually resolving to cherish each other the more, since they have no children of their own to care for (pp. 235–7).

Silas wants to return to North'ard to clear up the false accusation (pp. 237–8). When he arrives there with Eppie, however, the chapel has gone (pp. 239–40). He realizes that Raveloe is his real home. In spite of the past, Silas now has Eppie, his gold and his renewed faith in God and people (pp. 240–41). The novel ends with the village's celebration of Eppie's marriage to Aaron, after which the couple return with Silas to his cottage, where they make their home.

An Account of the Plot

PART ONE, CHAPTER 1, *pp. 51–62*

Country people of the nineteenth century, used to a society based on simple family life, were often suspicious of travelling weavers; the weavers' skill, knowledge and lack of family made them seem strange and even evil. Silas Marner, one such weaver, lives in a cottage by the edge of a stone-pit near the village of Raveloe. He is teased by the village lads and mistrusted by the country folk. For Raveloe lives an old-fashioned village life, away from the towns and centred on the church and those large families who make a living from farming, 'quite at their ease' (p. 54).

Silas has lived in Raveloe for fifteen years. He is a pale, short-sighted man from the industrial area of North'ard. From the start, Silas has not tried to fit into village life. He has not tried being neighbourly, meeting people at the inn or courting. What makes him even stranger is that Jem Rodney, the mole-catcher, has reported seeing Silas in a kind of fit one night. The villagers become convinced that this is the influence of the devil, particularly as the weaver seems to know how to cure illness with medicinal herbs.

In fact, Silas's life has been a sad one, and this accounts for his behaviour in Raveloe. When living in North'ard, he joined a fervent but narrow-minded religious community based around a chapel in Lantern Yard. The religion encouraged this 'young man of exemplary life' (p. 56) not to rely on himself but to place his faith wholeheartedly in a demanding God. Silas even gave up his practice of herbal medicine, which his mother had passed on to him. When he began to have mysterious fits of unconsciousness, these were seen not as illness but as a spiritual blessing, even though Silas could not remember having any visions during them.

The only criticism of Silas's behaviour came from his special friend, William Dane. This seemingly holy young man was convinced that God had chosen him to be saved, and he saw himself as superior to others in the chapel. William warned Silas that his fits might be the work of the devil. At the same time Silas's betrothed, Sarah, started behaving oddly towards him; sometimes very affectionately, sometimes coldly. However, since their engagement had been approved by the chapel, Sarah could offer no reason for breaking it off.

Caring for a sick church deacon during the night, Silas had one of his fits. He recovered to find that his patient had died, and that William, who had been supposed to relieve Silas at two o'clock, had not arrived. Fetching the minister, Silas went off to work. On his return he was summoned to Lantern Yard. There he was accused of stealing the chapel's money. His knife had been found in the drawer by the deacon's bedside, where the money was kept. William had apparently not arrived because of illness, so Silas was the only possible culprit.

Silas was amazed, but he trusted God to clear him of the false accusation. He suggested that his house be searched; when it was, William found the empty money-bag there. Suddenly, Silas remembered that the last time he had used the incriminating knife had been to help William cut a strap. He said nothing, again trusting that God would help him. According to the chapel custom, lots were drawn to find out the truth; and 'The lots declared that Silas Marner was guilty' (p. 61).

The innocent Silas then charged William with stealing the money and falsely accusing him. He also declared that God was neither just nor kind, and that he failed to help even innocent people. Silas felt his whole faith in God and humanity to have been turned upside down. Because of the influence of his religion he was unable to think rationally about what had occurred, however; and emotionally he could only respond in the extreme.

Next day, Sarah sent word through the minister that she wanted to end their engagement; but the final blow came just over a month later when Sarah and William got married. It was then that Silas left the town and went out into the countryside, finally settling in Raveloe.

When you read this first chapter of *Silas Marner*, try to assess how good an introduction to the book it is. Does it introduce you to the main character, his past life, his present problems? How far does it show the main ideas that George Eliot wants the reader to consider: the way people respond to each other and to God? Notice particularly the Lantern Yard episode and why it is included in this chapter. Finally, ask whether you are immediately involved in the book after starting to read.

CHAPTER 2, *pp. 62–70*

On leaving North'ard and coming to Raveloe, Silas feels he has entered a new but bitter life. The chapel at Lantern Yard had been the centre of his world. Raveloe, with its easy-going, materialistic attitudes, is very different. Silas can neither understand it nor find anything there to comfort him or restore him to his faith. He loses himself in his work, thinking of nothing beyond the present.

For this work, 'Silas was paid in gold' (p. 65). Money has never before been important to Silas. Now, for the first time, he has gold but no wish to share it with anyone or donate it to the church. Having no real use for it, he begins to regard gold as an end in itself. It is physically attractive to him, and he starts to save rather than spend it.

Silas is not liked by the people in Raveloe. At one point, however, he nearly finds acceptance. Taking his shoes to be mended, he sees that Sally Oates, the cobbler's wife, has the same symptoms of heart-disease and dropsy that his mother had shown. He brings Mrs Oates a herbal mixture that had helped his mother, and which helps her as well. Because of this kindness, Silas almost wants to mix with people and remember his past again. The villagers react with awe to his unusual skills, and compare him to a previous local figure, the witch-like Wise Woman (pp. 65–6).

Suddenly the weaver is besieged by people wanting cures. He is an honest man whose knowledge is limited, and he sends them away rather than take their money in return for useless mixtures. Because he will not cure them, people begin to think Silas is evil, and that he can harm as well as heal. They turn against him, and Silas withdraws yet again from village life to concentrate on his work and his gold. He spends each evening after work gloating over his wealth, and, although robbery is almost unknown in the village, he hides his coins away under the bricks near the loom.

Only one incident in fifteen years shows that Silas is still capable of genuine emotional response. He always uses a particular pot to fetch his water. When it breaks, he is greatly upset; he sticks the pieces together and props the pot in its usual place 'for a memorial' (p. 69). Otherwise Silas shows no sign of feeling for anything but his gold, which is like 'unborn children' to him (p. 70). He remains like this until the Christmas of his fifteenth year in Raveloe.

Chapter 2 covers the years Silas spends at Raveloe up to the main action of the story. He has changed during this time, which might affect your attitude towards him. Try to assess how far Silas is responsible for his faults, and how far Raveloe is to blame. Look, too, at what you have so far learnt about village life and how we are meant to judge the country folk.

CHAPTER 3, *pp. 71–82*

The Casses are the most important people in Raveloe. Their affluence is accepted, not resented, by poorer people, particularly as the Casses are generous when they hold celebrations. However, the peasants do criticize Squire Cass for not bringing up his motherless sons properly. Dunsey, the second son, is a scoundrel, and the eldest, Godfrey, appears to be 'going along the same road with his brother' (p. 73). He has even lost the favour of Nancy, daughter of another important Raveloe family, the Lammeters.

It is Godfrey who, fifteen years after Silas's arrival in Raveloe, is waiting in the parlour of his home, the Red House, to speak to his brother Dunsey. When Dunsey arrives it is obvious that he has some hold over Godfrey. Under pressure, Godfrey has previously lent Dunsey money. This is not his own, but rent collected from one of his father's tenants, which Godfrey should have handed to the Squire immediately. Now, thinking the rent unpaid, the Squire is threatening to repossess the tenant's land. Godfrey, eager to repay his father, wants Dunsey to return the money to him.

Confidently Dunsey tells Godfrey to find the money himself, perhaps by selling his horse Wildfire. Otherwise Dunsey will reveal the information with which he has been blackmailing his brother. He will make public Godfrey's secret: shameful marriage to drunken barmaid Molly Farren.

Godfrey at first calls his brother's bluff, threatening to tell the Squire everything himself. Thinking things over, however, he realizes that by doing so he would lose his father's approval, his inheritance, his place in the village and the slight chance of winning back Nancy Lammeter's favour, which he still hopes for despite his marriage.

Eventually Dunsey suggests that he himself take Godfrey's horse to a hunt the following day, sell him and regain the money. Godfrey will get a good price and will also be free to attend Mrs Osgood's party, where he plans to court Nancy. Unwillingly, Godfrey agrees. Dunsey is delighted and leaves in high spirits.

Godfrey, worried, stays behind. The author remarks that we tend to think of country squires as insensitive, dull and brutal, but that some, like Godfrey, are capable of finer feelings which they never altogether lose, and which lead them to suffer greatly. He has fallen – probably through Dunsey's plotting, he now realizes – into a marriage which is 'a blight on his life' (p. 80). His four-year courtship of Nancy has been wasted by this foolishness. Yet he still regards Nancy as a possible saviour who can offer him a pleasant, orderly family life. If only he can hide his marriage and dare to continue to court her, perhaps things will change for the better. Godfrey does not know how to do this, however, and he is becoming increasingly bitter about the situation. In the end he leaves for the Rainbow Inn to forget his troubles in idle chat.

Here, for the first time, we see upper-class Raveloe folk. How are we meant to judge them? This is an important scene, introducing us to Godfrey and Dunsey, their characters and their relationship. They both influence Silas. How? Godfrey's story parallels Silas's, and you might like to note any similarities you have perceived so far.

CHAPTER 4, *pp. 82–90*

Next morning Dunsey rides to the hunt near Batherley to sell Wildfire. He passes Silas's cottage on the way, and remembers talk of the miser's money. He immediately thinks of suggesting to Godfrey that he persuade the miser, by force if necessary, to lend him his hoard.

Arriving at the hunt Dunsey meets two acquaintances, Bryce and Keating (p. 83). To conceal his real intentions he tells them that he is riding Wildfire because Godfrey has given him the horse. Realizing he wants to sell, Bryce and Keating bargain with him for Wildfire, and Bryce eventually agrees to pay £120 for the horse later that day. Dunsey then joins the hunt, but, due to his drunkenness and poor judgement, he impales Wildfire on a hedge-stake when taking a fence. Not wanting to return to Batherley and the mockery of the others, he decides to return to Raveloe on foot, even though he is unused to long walks.

Returning home, Dunsey passes Silas's cottage and, seeing the light from the window, approaches the door. He has already decided that the only way to find the money to repay the Squire is to force Silas's gold from him. Finding the door of Marner's cottage unexpectedly open, Dunsey enters. Silas is not there. Dunsey warms himself at the fire. The opportunity for theft is too good to miss. He notices that the floor-bricks under the loom are the only ones not sprinkled with sand. They must have been moved. Lifting them, he discovers two leather bags, and 'what could there be but money' in them (p. 89)? Suddenly afraid, Dunsey leaves the cottage quickly and makes off 'into the darkness' (p. 90).

In this chapter we see the theft of the gold. The subject of money runs through all Dunsey's actions and thoughts. Dunsey dominates everything, and his villainous character is analysed in detail. What aspects of his personality are brought out particularly? Read the final sentence of the chapter carefully. What meaning might it have beyond the obvious one?

CHAPTER, 5 *pp. 90–95*

Meanwhile Silas is on his way back to the cottage, suspecting nothing. He has been out to fetch some twine for his weaving, leaving a rare treat, a bit of pork, roasting over the fire. Because Silas is using the door-key as part of the makeshift spit on which to roast the pork, he had to choose between locking the door and cooking the meat. He chose the latter, which explains why the cottage door was open.

On his return Silas does not notice anything amiss, and starts warming himself by the fire. In its light, his face takes on a fearful appearance, but 'few men could be more harmless'; despite his love of gold, the author explains, Silas has still a 'truthful simple soul' (p. 92).

Silas goes to take out his guineas to look at them over dinner. He finds them gone; he stops to think, examines the empty hole again, looks round the room and at last has to face the truth. He gives 'a wild ringing scream, the cry of desolation' (p. 93). He turns to his loom for consolation, gradually realizing that, unless some spirit has been at work, a thief must have taken his gold. Perhaps Jem Rodney the poacher, who one day lingered by Silas's fire for a while, is the man.

Silas decides to go to the Rainbow Inn to find the important people in the village – the Squire, the clergyman and the constable – who will help him.

After the theft of the gold, we see Silas's reaction to it. What do we learn from this about his character and his love of the gold? Notice in particular any similarities or differences between Silas's love of gold and Dunsey's, and between his reaction to the theft and the reaction of the Lantern Yard community to the theft they suffer. What effect does his loss have on Silas? Does he still reject God and other people now he no longer has the gold?

CHAPTER 6, *pp. 95–105*

When the villagers meet that evening in the Rainbow, everyone is at first quiet. Then Mr Lundy, the butcher, and the farrier, Mr Dowlas, start to disagree about a cow brought in for slaughter. The landlord tries to make the peace, and turns the conversation by appealing to Mr Macey, the tailor and parish clerk. This leads to more cutting remarks, this time directed towards Mr Tookey, Macey's deputy. Tookey is also insulted by Ben Winthrop, the wheelwright, who as leader of the church choir accuses the deputy of being unable to sing. Once more, the landlord has to intervene to keep the peace.

Mr Macey is encouraged to tell some of his well-known tales, firstly about the Lammeter family coming to the area, settling in easily and being accepted. In fact the young Mr Lammeter even married the young Miss Osgood, although the service itself was irregular: the parson got the words the wrong way round. No one noticed but Mr Macey, who thought that the wedding might be null and void until the parson set his mind at rest.

Mr Macey's next tale concerns Mr Cliff, another stranger to the area. Cliff, who came from London, never fitted in. A tailor, he was not proud of his profession as Mr Macey is of his, but aspired to higher social status. He tried to ride, built over-large stables and drove his son to his death. Now, the country folk say, his ghost walks. This turns the conversation to the supernatural. Mr Dowlas challenges anyone to a nocturnal watch at the stables with him. Everyone is wary of this suggestion, however, since unlike Dowlas they believe in the spirit world. The landlord, again attempting to pacify them, suggests as a compromise that some are more sensitive than others to the presence of ghosts.

We meet the villagers for the first time in this scene, though none save Mr Macey is developed as a character. What do we learn about them, especially about their attitude to strangers? Look at Mr Macey's two stories for help with this.

This chapter acts as light relief between two more serious ones. Ask yourself how its humour works, and how appropriate it is to this stage of the novel. Was George Eliot right to place it here, or does it distract from the main story?

CHAPTER 7, *pp. 106–11*

Suddenly Silas Marner appears as if from nowhere, like the ghosts the villagers have been discussing. Everyone is startled. The landlord approaches him, and Silas gasps out the news: 'I've been robbed!' (p. 106). He turns on Jem Rodney and asks him to return the money at once. In response to this seemingly mad accusation Jem is naturally angry. The landlord makes Silas sit down and tell his story. The country people believe him almost at once. They are sensitive enough to perceive that he would not be so bewildered and 'mushed' (p. 108) were he lying.

Their first conclusion is that some unknown, possibly ghostly being has committed the theft. Certainly it was not Jem Rodney. Silas, seeing how unjust he has been in his accusation, apologizes at once to the mole-catcher: 'I don't accuse you – I won't accuse anybody' (p. 109). The villagers next wonder if a tramp could be the thief, and lastly action is decided on. Silas must go to the constable, who is at present ill in bed. After some argument about who should accompany him, the landlord and the farrier do so.

When Silas turns to the villagers for help, we learn more about both him and them. Compare, for instance, the villagers' reaction to that of the chapel community. George Eliot hints that Silas has already begun to change because of the country folk's attitude to him. What evidence of this do you find?

CHAPTER 8, *pp. 111–20*

The news of the robbery causes great excitement in the village. No one, not even Godfrey, suspects Dunsey, who has not yet returned home. Some think that Silas might have arranged the theft himself; Mr Macey believes supernatural forces are responsible. A tinder-box is found near Silas's house, and Mr Snell remembers seeing a pedlar with a tinder-box in the district a month before. Being an outsider the pedlar is immediately suspect, and any evidence of his unusualness (such as wearing ear-rings) is seen as proof of his guilt. All the villagers tell their own embroidered and exaggerated stories about him. Silas's inability to recall any untoward behaviour on the pedlar's part when he visited his cottage, therefore, causes a certain amount of disappointment.

Meanwhile, Godfrey is far more concerned about what has happened to Dunsey and Wildfire. He rides off in the direction of Batherley to try and find his brother. On the way he meets Bryce, who tells him that Dunsey sold the horse to him but then killed it on a staked hedge. Out of pride, Godfrey will not admit that Dunsey did all this against his wishes. He is afraid that Bryce will go to the Red House and tell the Squire everything, but Bryce rides away having said that no doubt Dunsey has disappeared until the news about Wildfire dies down.

Godfrey returns home. He knows now that he cannot pay his father, and that he will have to confess what has happened. By the evening he has determined to tell the truth. After all, Molly herself might appear at any moment and carry out her threat to betray him. Godfrey's only chance is that his father's pride will prefer keeping the affair quiet to publicizing it by turning him out. By next morning, though, Godfrey is again frightened by all the disadvantages of confession. If Dunsey does not come back for a while, he tells himself, 'everything might blow over' (p. 120).

The two parts of this chapter deal with the effects of the theft on the villagers and on Godfrey. Again, compare the villagers' response with that of the Lantern Yard community. Notice, too, how we learn about Godfrey's character, particularly when he talks himself into and out of confession. You should by now have a clear idea of the faults in his personality.

CHAPTER 9, *pp. 120–27*

Godfrey waits for his father after breakfast. The Squire is an untidy man, but nevertheless has an air of authority that makes him seem more important than the villagers. He greets his son harshly and rebukes him for his laziness. Godfrey begins to break the news about Wildfire; thinking Godfrey is asking for a loan because of the mishap, the Squire is quick to mention that he is as 'short o' cash as a roadside pauper' (p. 121). Godfrey then admits that Dunsey has killed Wildfire while taking him to be sold to repay Fowler's money.

The Squire is at first astonished, then purple with rage at Godfrey's taking his tenant's rent and Dunsey's foolishness with the horse. He threatens to cut off his sons' inheritance by remarrying, then demands to see Dunsey at once. Godfrey tells him Dunsey is not back yet, and the Squire sees there is something between the two brothers. 'You've been up to some trick, and you've been bribing him not to tell' (p. 124).

Godfrey is startled by his father's correct guess, but manages to side-step the question, and the Squire soon starts to complain about money again. Why does Godfrey not act like a man and help him with the estate? Why does he not marry Nancy and start a family of his own to carry on the Cass name? When Godfrey hesitates, the Squire actually offers to make the marriage proposal for him. This, of course, is the last thing Godfrey wants. He tries to dissuade his father by telling him that Nancy seems unsure about marriage. By this time the Squire is calmer. He orders Godfrey to sell Dunsey's horse to make up Fowler's money and to tell his brother, when he sees him, not to bother to come home.

Godfrey is relieved that the worst has not happened, but he is now even more trapped by his lies. His last resort, as always, is to place his trust in 'blessed Chance' (p. 127), believing that, though it is through his own fault that he is in this awkward position, some favourable turn of fortune will come to his aid.

We have now seen Godfrey with his father. What criticisms does George Eliot make of rich country folk in general and of the Squire in particular? Is he a good father, and how have his attitudes affected Godfrey? What do we learn about Godfrey from the way he responds to his father and to the situation? Notice lastly that because of the Squire's orders nobody bothers searching for Dunsey, so that his body lies undiscovered for years.

CHAPTER 10, *pp. 127–43*

In spite of an inquiry the pedlar suspected of taking Silas's money is not found, and the excitement over the affair dies away. Dunsey does not turn up again, but no one seems concerned, and no one links his disappearance with the robbery. Silas, though, has lost his reason for living: when the gold was taken, 'the support was snatched away' (p. 129). He grieves for the loss as if it were that of a living being. The villagers try to help him. They are sympathetic, send him Christmas food, stop to talk to him and call at his house. Their condolences often upset Silas even more, but they are well meant.

Two people in particular try to help. Mr Macey visits and rambles on as usual, remarking graciously that in place of his original distrust he now regards the weaver as harmless. To be fully restored to village favour, however, Macey suggests that Silas attend church and 'be a bit neighbourly' (p. 132). Silas cannot really respond to these well-meant words, and later, at the Rainbow, Mr Macey comments that Silas is so confused he would not even know when Sunday was; which shows him to be 'a worse heathen than many a dog' (p. 133).

Dolly Winthrop, the wheelwright's wife, a good-hearted, hard-working, 'wholesome woman' (p. 134), also visits Silas one Sunday to offer him some lard-cakes she has made. She points out the 'good letters' (p. 136) on them, which she cannot read, but which she believes she must prick out when she bakes cakes, to bless them.

Dolly then turns the talk to church, suggesting that Silas should go one Sunday: 'you'd be a deal the better,' she tells him (p. 137). Silas astonishes Dolly by saying he knows nothing about 'church'. Lantern Yard was a chapel, and he does not really understand the word 'church'. Dolly's advice is more confusing than helpful, therefore, since Silas cannot relate it to his limited experience of religion at Lantern Yard.

Dolly hopes to influence Silas through Aaron, her son. She is sure that Silas will take to the child and so begin to respond to people again. What Dolly does not know is that the short-sighted Silas can hardly see the little boy, and that the carol Aaron sings means nothing to him because he has never heard carols before. Dolly leaves with a final plea to Silas to stop working on Sundays and to attend church.

Silas is still too affected by his past and by the theft of his gold to understand Dolly: 'his soul was still the shrunken rivulet'. He spends Christmas 'in loneliness, eating his meat in sadness of heart' (p. 140), thinking neither of going to church nor of seeing other people. In Raveloe itself, the festival is celebrated merrily; at Squire Cass's all is jolly, and no one mentions Dunsey at all.

The Christmas celebration at the Red House is far less important than the traditional dance at New Year. This year Godfrey is torn between looking forward to a happy evening with Nancy and worrying that Dunsey will return, that Molly needs more money and that the Squire will force him into a proposal of marriage. If these things happen, all will be lost.

Chapter 10 shows us the long-term effects of the theft on Silas. How does his misery alter our attitude towards him? The villagers, too, are affected, and we learn more about them because of this. In particular notice the scene where Dolly first visits Silas. What differences between city and country, church and chapel, are highlighted here? Finally, compare Godfrey's predicament, described at the close of the chapter, with that of Silas. How are their problems similar, how different? How is each responsible for his misery?

CHAPTER 11, *pp. 143–63*

Nancy Lammeter arrives at the Casses' New Year's Eve party, riding behind her father but nevertheless looking bewitchingly beautiful. She dreads being lifted down from the horse by Godfrey, however, since her feelings towards him are confused. First he courted her, then he ignored her, and now he is courting her again. But on arriving at the Red House Nancy remains calm as he lifts her down. She hurries indoors.

Entering the Blue Room to dress, Nancy meets her aunt, Mrs Osgood, and is introduced to some of the other ladies. She opens her box, which is neat and pretty to perfection, and dresses herself. Nancy looks beautiful even though her hands are rough from housework and she speaks with a country accent. Her honesty and refinement make her a lady in spite of her lack of education.

Nancy's sister Priscilla arrives, a 'cheerful-looking lady' (p. 148) who chatters on about her wish to be independent of men. Priscilla is concerned about wearing an identical outfit to Nancy's; the younger girl has insisted on this because she wants the two to look like sisters, but the result is not flattering to Priscilla. The older girl urges Nancy to look around and choose a husband, since Godfrey has let her down. Priscilla is happy to remain unmarried, but there is no reason for Nancy to do the same.

Everyone goes in to tea. Nancy is seated next to Godfrey, which embarrasses her. She is determined not to marry him because his behaviour is irresponsible and inconsistent, but she is also not prepared to love anyone else: '"love once, love always"' (p. 151). Her embarrassed blush is noticed by the village Rector, who compliments her on her colour, as does the Squire. Mr Lammeter, though pleased at the attention being paid to his daughter, is thinking that Godfrey must improve before he can hope to marry her.

Dr Kimble joins in the conversation, praising Priscilla for her cooking and asking Nancy to save a dance for him. The Squire encourages Godfrey to ask Nancy for a dance as well, and he does so uncomfortably. Nancy agrees, though she tries to act as coldly towards Godfrey as possible.

The dancing begins almost as soon as Solomon, Mr Macey's brother and the best fiddler in the area, appears, playing a country tune. Everyone moves into the White Parlour for dancing, and the Squire leads off opposite the Rector. The dancers are watched by a few privileged villagers; among them Mr Macey and Ben Winthrop, who pass comment on the gentry, sometimes critically. They notice that Nancy and Godfrey seem to be 'sweethearting' (p. 160) again, for they walk off into the parlour together.

In fact Nancy's dress has caught under the Squire's foot, and she is simply going to wait for Priscilla to come and mend it. Godfrey takes the opportunity to declare that 'one dance with you matters more to me than all the other pleasures in the world' (p. 162). Nancy is startled, but not wishing to reveal her true feelings replies coldly. Godfrey promises to make amends for his past behaviour, but Nancy again answers sternly and they almost quarrel. Godfrey sees it as a victory that there is at least some emotion left in Nancy's attitude towards him.

Their conversation is interrupted by Priscilla, come to mend the dress. By this time, however, Godfrey feels reckless. He stays to enjoy Nancy's company regardless of the consequences.

This celebratory scene at the Red House contrasts with the next, tragic chapter. We learn more about Raveloe gentry, particularly Nancy, whom we meet for the first time. What impression do you have of her character, and how is Godfrey's personality revealed by his behaviour towards her? Ask yourself whether, at this point in the book, you like Nancy Lammeter.

CHAPTER 12, *pp. 163–9*

Molly, Godfrey's wife, is walking to Raveloe with her child in her arms. She has determined to revenge her misery by exposing Godfrey, who is enjoying himself at the Red House party and 'hiding *her* existence in the darkest corner of his heart' (p. 163). The cause of

Molly's unhappiness is in reality her addiction to opium, and she knows it; in her wretchedness, though, her confused mind is bitter because the wealthy Godfrey, regretting the marriage, leaves her penniless.

Molly has waited on the road because of the heavily falling snow, and it is now dark and late. She does not know how much further she has to go, although in fact she is close to Raveloe. She takes out the drug, hesitates, then drinks. She walks on, feeling increasingly numb. All she wants is to sleep. At last she sinks down, still clutching her baby, and slips into unconsciousness.

After a while, 'the fingers lost their tension, the arms unbent' (p. 165); the baby wakes and, looking round, sees a bright light. It toddles after it. The light is that of Silas's fire, which the baby sees through the open door of the cottage. Silas, jokingly advised by the villagers to sit up and watch the New Year in, has opened the door; he has become used to doing so in the forlorn hope of hearing passing news of his gold. As he opens the door, he slips into one of his trances. The baby toddles into the cottage, goes over to the warmth of the fire and falls asleep in front of it without Silas noticing anything.

When Silas recovers and looks round, he sees at first only the baby's hair gleaming in the firelight, and thinks it is 'his own gold – brought back to him as mysteriously as it had been taken away!' (p. 167). He is overcome with joy. But the golden glow, when he touches it, proves to be a baby's hair. Confused, he believes the child to be his dead sister, whom he looked after when he was young. Then he sees that the child is a stranger, and wonders how it came to be there. He finds himself starting to feel emotions he has not felt since his time at Lantern Yard: 'old quiverings of tenderness' and a renewed sense of God's part in his life (p. 168).

The child wakes up; Marner comforts her, then feeds her and removes her wet, uncomfortable boots. They remind him that the child must have come through the snow from somewhere, and he thinks to look outside. He finds the baby's mother under the furze bushes, half-covered with snow.

This chapter is in complete contrast to the previous one. How does the cold, dark, threatening atmosphere of its first half reflect what is happening? The scene where Molly abandons responsibility for the child by taking the drug is particularly important, and may remind you of the later scene where Godfrey too refuses to take responsibility for the baby. Which parent is more to blame?

When the infant enters Silas's cottage, the atmosphere changes. Why? Also, consider why the baby is immediately likened to Silas's gold. What is this meant to show us about her part in his life? Finally, you might like to consider the coincidence involved when the child enters the cottage unnoticed. Why do you think George Eliot wrote the tale in this way?

CHAPTER 13, *pp. 170–77*

At the Red House the dancing continues. Godfrey is watching Nancy, but is careful not to approach so near that his father will be able to make further remarks about marriage. Suddenly he looks up to see 'his own child carried in Silas Marner's arms' (p. 171).

Silas's appearance creates a commotion. He reports that there is a woman, almost certainly dead, at the Stone-pits near his house. Godfrey is afraid: afraid that Molly may not be dead and afraid that he may now have to admit that she is his wife.

Mrs Kimble, the doctor's wife, offers to take the baby, but Silas refuses to part with it. 'It's come to me,' he says, '– I've a right to keep it' (p. 172). This is the first time he has considered keeping the baby, but he feels suddenly impelled to do so. The doctor appears and asks for Dolly Winthrop's help before setting off back to the Stone-pits with Silas.

Godfrey, keen to see his wife's condition for himself, fetches Dolly and goes with her to Silas's cottage. Ironically, Dolly thanks Godfrey for his goodness in coming out in the cold. His only emotion is the hope that Molly is dead and that his troubles are over. Deep down, he is conscious of his guilt in this, and inwardly promises that if his wishes come true he will 'be a good fellow in future' (p. 174) and ensure that the child is cared for.

The doctor emerges from the cottage with the news that the woman is indeed dead, and Godfrey makes an excuse to go in and look at her. The child is there as well, in Silas's arms. She returns Godfrey's gaze without recognition. He decides then not to reveal that she is his child. She turns and pulls at Silas's cheek affectionately (p. 175). When Godfrey learns that Silas wants to keep the child, he gives him a little money towards clothing her and then sets off for home. When questioned, he explains away his unusual action in going to the cottage by more lies.

By the time he reaches the Red House, Godfrey is feeling greatly relieved. He may now safely court Nancy. Even if Dunsey returns, he can be 'won to silence' (p. 177). Godfrey once again justifies his actions with the thought that he, Nancy and the child will surely be happier like this, and that such a welcome result must reflect well on his own actions.

Having seen Silas's reactions to the child and mother, we now see those of Godfrey. His desire for Molly's death and his refusal to acknowledge his baby are Godfrey's worst deeds, so examine these scenes carefully. They affect both his character and the later action of the book in many ways. Look also at his rejection by the child, which should remind you of a scene later in the book.

Silas, on the other hand, has taken a great step forward. What is it, and how does it affect his character?

CHAPTER 14, *pp. 178–91*

In the same week, Molly has a pauper's burial in Raveloe. At her lodgings in Batherley they know only that she has left, and so her life ends unnoticed, though it has greatly affected others.

Everyone is surprised that Silas has decided to keep the child, and they are not slow to give sympathy and advice. Dolly Winthrop offers to come and help Silas with the baby, whose strange arrival she describes as being like the great rhythms of life: we have no control over them, and little understanding of them. Realizing that Silas wants to care for the child himself, Dolly tactfully remarks that the baby is 'fondest o' you' (p. 180). Then she shows him the right way to dress and look after her. Silas suggests that while he is working the little one be kept safe by being tied to the leg of the loom, and Dolly agrees.

One thing Dolly insists upon is that the child be christened and learn her catechism. This, she says, will keep the baby safe, like inoculation. Silas concurs because he wants to do 'whatever's right for it i' this country' (p. 182). He suggests the name Hephzibah, the name of his mother and sister, shortened to Eppie. Dolly is delighted at his compliance, and the christening is soon arranged. Silas goes to church for the first time then, although he hardly understands this kind of service.

As Eppie grows, so does her influence on Silas. Unlike his gold, she loves and responds to nature, to people and to life. Unlike the gold, too, she changes and develops. Her demands on Silas slowly make him similarly aware of the world. He starts to look forward to the future with something like happiness, and to remember the past; for Eppie is 're-awakening his senses with her fresh life' (p. 184).

But of course the older Eppie grows, the more wayward she becomes. Dolly suggests smacking her or shutting her in the coal-hole. Silas does not want to punish her for fear she should love him the less for it. One day, however, while Silas is busy at work, Eppie creeps over, steals the scissors, cuts the cloth that ties her to the loom, and runs out of the cottage. Finding Eppie gone, Silas is terrified in case she has been hurt. He eventually discovers her sitting in a drained pond, covered in mud.

Silas is relieved and happy to see the child, but once they arrive home he realizes that she should be punished to '"make her remember"' (p. 187); if she runs away again, she might be hurt. He puts Eppie in the coal-hole, but only for a moment, not wanting to upset her and thinking that this will be enough. Then he washes her and changes her clothes. Eppie immediately runs back into the coal-hole, delighted with the new game. Thereafter, Silas makes up his mind not to punish her, and Dolly sympathetically agrees. Eppie is brought up without 'frowns and denials' (p. 189), and Silas works hard to keep her out of mischief. His life now revolves round Eppie. Gold seems irrelevant. The child is like an angel, rescuing him from his old state of mind and leading him away from the 'threatening destruction' (p. 191) of his obsession.

Chapter 14 shows us Silas beginning life as a foster-parent. Notice how his character changes through his love for the baby, and how the villagers' attitude to him also changes. What part does Dolly play here? Also look at the kind of baby Eppie is, and compare her with the adult she has become in Chapter 16. What does this show you about Silas and his role as a parent? Is he better or worse than other parents in the book?

CHAPTER 15, *pp. 191–2*

Godfrey is watching Eppie grow. He only feels able to help her with small gifts from time to time, in case his charity arouses suspicion. But he consoles himself that the child is probably happier with Silas than living in luxury with him. He courts Nancy again, and she is now happy to encourage him, for he seems to have turned over a new leaf. Godfrey confidently looks forward to marrying and raising his own family. He promises himself that when this happens he will take care of Eppie: 'That was a father's duty' (p. 192).

This chapter concludes Part One of the book. We have seen Silas and Eppie happily settled, and we turn to Godfrey. He seems content, but is there any hint that his future will not be as happy as he expects?

PART TWO, CHAPTER 16, *pp. 195–210*

Sixteen years later, the villagers are leaving church one autumn Sunday. Godfrey seems older. Nancy, now his wife, has changed more than he, but is still lovely because she has kept and increased her goodness. The couple are with Mr Lammeter and Priscilla.

Silas and Eppie are at church too. Silas now looks old, but Eppie has grown into the 'freshest blossom of youth' (p. 196), a beautiful girl of eighteen much admired by Aaron Winthrop. Eppie tells Silas how she wants a garden outside the cottage, but she is worried the work will be too hard for him. Aaron offers to do the work, and even to bring cuttings from other gardens in the village, where he is a gardener, for there is always enough to go round if people are willing to share.

Silas and Eppie, delighted with Aaron's offer, return home. The cottage is now well kept and homely. Silas's life has improved, with help from the villagers, especially Godfrey, and he is now wholly accepted in Raveloe. They eat, then Silas goes out to smoke his pipe.

Silas has changed during the intervening years. Gradually he has been able to think again of the time at Lantern Yard and even to tell Dolly what happened. She is shocked by the story, and it is a source of great perplexity to her until, sitting up with a dying village woman one night, she concludes that the God who created us must be wiser and more loving than we are; the one thing she is certain of, therefore, is that we must trust in 'Them above', and that 'there's a good and a rights bigger nor what we can know' (p. 204). Silas agrees, though he finds it hard to have faith. He perceives that there must be a divinity because, in spite of all his suffering, Eppie has been sent to him.

When she was young, Silas told Eppie the story of how she came to him and showed her the wedding-ring that had belonged to her mother. Eppie does not ask herself who her father was, for she has Silas: 'a father very close to her' (p. 206). She often thinks about her mother, though. Today, planning her garden, she wants to include in it the furze bush where her mother was found, and Silas agrees to this. The girl tries to carry stones for the garden boundary, but they are too heavy for her. She and Silas sit for a while in silence.

Eppie then reveals that Aaron has asked her to marry him. Silas is startled, but tries to hide his fear that Eppie will leave him. Aaron is ready to marry, has a good job and, Eppie tells him, is eager for the three of them to stay together as a family. Eppie likes Aaron, as does

Silas, but in many ways 'I'd sooner things didn't change' (p. 209). Silas thinks Eppie is young to be married, but knows that he is getting older and will soon be dependent on her. It would be good for her to have a strong young man to lean on. They agree to ask Dolly's advice, for she will be able to decide what is the right thing to do.

This chapter describes the situation sixteen years after the end of Part One. How has everyone changed? In particular, how has Silas changed in his attitudes to God and to other people? Examine his relationship with Eppie and compare it with other parent–child relationships in the book. Notice that Aaron is introduced here, so that when Eppie decides to marry him later we know what kind of life she is choosing.

CHAPTER 17, *pp. 210–21*

Godfrey and Nancy are finishing lunch at the Red House. Nancy is eager for her guests, Priscilla and Mr Lammeter, to stay longer. Priscilla, though, now in charge of her father's house, insists they return home. The two sisters walk in the garden, and Priscilla comments that it is good that Godfrey is draining land near the Stone-pits in order to start dairying. It will keep Nancy busy and therefore more contented. Nancy replies that she wishes it would make Godfrey happy, for he is 'disappointed at not having any children' (p. 213). This exasperates Priscilla, though Nancy defends her husband.

As the guests leave, Godfrey sets off for his usual Sunday walk, and Nancy sits down to read her Bible and ponder all she has recently said and done. As always, she is concerned about Godfrey, wondering if she is to blame for his restlessness. The fact that they have no children makes them both unhappy, and particularly Godfrey. Nancy believes that she should not question what God has ordained, so she tries not to be upset. She has even stopped brooding over the drawer of baby's clothes which she still keeps after the death of her one child. She does, however, ask herself whether she has done 'everything in her power to lighten Godfrey's privation' (p. 216).

She can think of only one thing. Godfrey has suggested adopting Eppie. But Nancy is convinced that if they do, and so 'choose [their] lot in spite of Providence' (p. 216), they will be inviting misfortune. Godfrey himself has no real idea of what taking the child from Silas would mean, regarding labourers as people with few deep feelings. Eppie's material benefit, he feels, will be sufficient reason for Silas to surrender her. Godfrey is a naturally kind person, however, and Nancy is right to think that he has been good to her over the past years, in spite of his disappointment. Godfrey also perceives that Nancy's refusal to adopt Eppie is not selfish stubbornness, but 'an unselfish clinging to thc right' (p. 219). Nancy does not yet know the truth about Eppie. Godfrey is convinced that if he told his wife about the past he would lose her – the very last thing he wants – but his desire for children still causes him distracting dissatisfaction. Finally, Nancy's thoughts turn to the future. How will Godfrey feel as he grows older and has no family to support him and to inherit his land?

Nancy's thoughts are interrupted by the maid bringing in the tea with the news that something has happened, for people are rushing past the window. Nancy feels uneasy at this, and waits anxiously for Godfrey to return.

We now see Godfrey and Nancy's position after sixteen years. Why do you think we look particularly at Nancy's point of view here? Neither she nor Godfrey is happy, but for slightly different reasons. You might like to contrast them with each other, and with Priscilla, who though childless still seems happy. How much do you sympathize with Nancy now, and has your opinion of her changed since Chapter 11?

CHAPTER 18, *pp. 221–5*

Godfrey returns, but Nancy's welcome is cut short by the shock on his face. He warns her that he has bad news, and at first she thinks it concerns her family. Then Godfrey tells her that Dunsey's skeleton has been found at the bottom of the drained Stone-pit. Silas's gold was with him, proving that Dunsey stole the money. Nancy is shaken by the news and is also ashamed, on her own behalf and on Godfrey's, that such a crime should be committed by someone in the family.

Dunsey's death has revealed to Godfrey that 'Everything comes to light . . . sooner or later' (p. 223) if God so wishes. Godfrey is afraid Nancy might discover the truth after he is dead, and decides to tell her about his marriage and about Eppie.

Nancy looks down without replying when Godfrey has finished his confession, and he is convinced that she will leave and never forgive him. Then his wife says simply that she wishes she had known before, since they could then have adopted Eppie earlier. As she is Godfrey's child, it would not have been defying Providence. Both Godfrey and Nancy would have been happier with a child to love, and 'our life might have been more like what we used to think it 'ud be' (p. 224).

Godfrey apprehends that 'He had not measured this wife with whom he had lived so long' (p. 224). He need not have lived a lie all these years. But had he told her earlier, perhaps Nancy would never have forgiven him. She replies that she does not know what would have happened, but that one thing is certain. Nothing is worth doing wrong for. 'Nothing is as good as it seems beforehand – not even our marrying wasn't, you see' (p. 224), she tells him. Nancy forgives Godfrey fully, though she reminds him that he has done wrong to Eppie. Godfrey suggests that, although after all these years it will not be the same, they should now adopt the girl. Nancy agrees, and they decide to go to see Silas that night.

The novel is now nearing its climax. The discovery of Dunsey's body results in Godfrey's decision to tell Nancy the truth and to adopt Eppie. Godfrey's character does indeed undergo change here. In what ways does it do so, and why? Does he, from now on, always act selflessly? Nancy too rises in our estimation, and you might like to review her character in the light of what you learn here.

PLOT

This chapter prepares us for the next, putting us in a state of suspense by giving us cause for concern about Silas. His life with Eppie is now at risk. Will Godfrey succeed in taking Eppie from Silas, just as Dunsey took his gold?

CHAPTER 19, *pp. 225–35*

That evening, Silas is alone with Eppie in their cottage, still tense with excitement after the discovery of the gold. The money is on the table in front of them while Silas tells Eppie how it was stolen and how she replaced it in his affection. It means nothing to him now. He is only afraid of losing her, and of losing the feeling that 'God was good to me' (p. 226).

Suddenly there is a knock on the door and Godfrey and Nancy enter. Godfrey apologizes to Silas for Dunsey's theft of the gold. He does not mention immediately that he is Eppie's father, hoping not to have to reveal this. Godfrey reminds Silas that he will soon have to stop his work as a weaver because of his age. He has hardly enough money to support Eppie and himself. Surely Silas would be pleased to see his daughter well provided for?

Silas is insulted, but Godfrey does not notice this and goes on to suggest that he and Nancy adopt Eppie. While Godfrey is talking, Eppie puts a supporting arm around Silas, who fears most of all that she might welcome the offer. He tells her to answer Godfrey as she wishes. Eppie curtsies to the Casses, and tells them that she will not leave her father or the village life she has been used to.

Silas is greatly relieved. Nancy is sympathetic to Eppie but upset for her husband. Godfrey is angry that he is not allowed to make amends and do the good he wants to. He does not understand the strength of Silas's and Eppie's feelings for each other or how much it would hurt Silas if Eppie were taken away. Godfrey therefore declares his claim to Eppie, hoping to put pressure on Silas: 'She's my own child: her mother was my wife' (p. 230).

Eppie is deeply shocked. Silas, having heard her refuse Godfrey's offer, feels secure enough to allow himself to be angry. He demands to know why Godfrey is making his claim now, when Eppie and he have lived and loved as father and daughter for so many years. Godfrey in return accuses the weaver of selfishness: 'You're putting yourself in the way of her welfare' (p. 232).

Eventually, desiring what is best for Eppie because of his love for her, Silas relents: 'Speak to the child. I'll hinder nothing' (p. 232).

Even Nancy at this point feels that it can only be to Eppie's advantage to become a Cass. Godfrey appeals to his daughter, reminding her of the benefits she will gain and trying to reassure her that Silas will always be cared for.

Eppie, knowing how Silas feels and repelled by Godfrey, replies firmly. She refuses his offer again and affirms her grateful love for Silas. She will never regret not having fine things, for they would distance her from the people she loves.

Nancy reminds her of her daughterly duty, but Eppie answers that she cannot think of anyone but Silas as her father, and she is doing her duty to him. Finally, she announces that she is 'promised to a working-man' (p. 234); she chooses her place in life with Silas and the villagers.

Godfrey is speechless with disappointment. He goes to the door and Nancy is left to say good-bye to Silas and Eppie, promising that they will meet again.

This chapter is the climax of the novel, and you need to approach it in several different ways. Ask first what you learn about the four main characters, their strengths and their weaknesses. Compare Godfrey to Silas, Nancy to Eppie, and their reactions to the challenge. Notice how the main themes are examined: family, money, the triumph of good over evil. Ask yourself what George Eliot is trying to tell us about the right way to live. Finally, consider how affected you are by the chapter. Does it involve you and make you concerned about the outcome, particularly for Silas Marner?

CHAPTER 20, *pp. 235–7*

Nancy and Godfrey return home. They realize that 'That's ended' (p. 235) and hug each other. Godfrey now knows Silas was right. He himself must bear with the consequences of his actions. Because of the past, Eppie will never truly love him. Godfrey decides, much to Nancy's relief, not to tell anyone of the affair, but to reveal it in his will. He further decides that he must make Eppie happy 'in her own way' (p. 236), rather than in the way he himself thinks best for her. He must help her to be happy in village life. Finally, Godfrey regrets ever being dissatisfied with his lot. After all, he has Nancy, and he resolves that a little resignation on his part will enhance their remaining years together.

For Godfrey and Nancy the story ends here. They accept that their family will never be complete, and they try to help each other. Both characters have by this stage demonstrated their good points. How have they developed throughout the book? How contented are they by the end, and do they deserve what happens to them?

CHAPTER 21, *pp. 237–41*

For Silas there is one last thing to do. He suggests to Eppie that they revisit Lantern Yard. Eppie is pleased at the prospect of 'seeing a strange country' (p. 238), and Dolly is glad that Silas will know whether the truth about the theft and the drawing of lots has come to light.

The pair arrive in North'ard. Silas is bemused by the changes that have occurred in his absence, and Eppie feels 'as if I was stifled' (p. 239). Eventually they reach the right district, only to find that Lantern Yard has been replaced by a factory. Silas is distressed, and Eppie takes him into nearby shop to recover. He can find no trace of the chapel community.

Back in Raveloe, Silas tells Dolly that 'I've no home but this now' (p. 240). He will never know whether he has been cleared of the theft, or understand what happened when the lots were drawn. Dolly comforts him by saying it does not matter, and Silas agrees that he can trust in the benevolence of God. Now that he knows Eppie will never leave him, he is sure 'I shall trusten till I die' (p. 241).

We learn a great deal from this chapter; in what the Lantern Yard episode shows us, for example. What lesson does Silas learn here about trust? This is also the point in the book to consider what your final feelings about Silas are, and how George Eliot wishes us to see him.

CONCLUSION, *pp. 241–4*

Springtime is the best time for Raveloe weddings, and in the spring Eppie marries. After the wedding she walks into the village between Silas and Aaron, with Dolly and Ben behind. Godfrey is away, but Nancy has given Eppie a wedding-dress, and Priscilla and Mr Lammeter see the procession as they call at the Red House. The villagers and Mr Macey welcome the wedding party, commenting that Silas has 'brought a blessing on himself by acting like a father' (p. 243) to Eppie. At the Rainbow Ben turns aside, and it is Silas, Dolly, Aaron and Eppie who go on to the cottage, where, as they enter their new life, Eppie declares that 'nobody could be happier than we are' (p. 244).

The conclusion to *Silas Marner* brings together every character and idea in the book. Look at how the main characters are shown, and how this reflects their place in the novel. We are shown how human love and acceptance in society are blessed by God's church, and the marriage of Eppie and Aaron celebrates this triumph of goodness over the forces of greed and despair.

Characters

SILAS MARNER

The story of Silas's life, his trials and his joys, form the focus of our interest and sympathy throughout the novel. We know very little about him as a child, however. He was brought up in the town, and must have been poor, 'a small boy without shoes or stockings' (p. 168). There is no mention of his father, but his mother seems to have been a kindly woman, skilled in herbal remedies. Perhaps she came from the country to the town to look for work. Silas had a generous heart, and took care of his little sister until her early death. He became a weaver, a craftsman, and must have been skilled to do this, although in general he seems quite simple in his approach to things.

Silas soon finds a religious group to join: Lantern Yard, where he makes friends and meets Sarah, his prospective wife. Like many in the community, he relies heavily on the directions and rules of the chapel, and does not readily develop any 'independent thought' (p. 62). He also starts having fits, a sign of his increasing nervousness. Nevertheless, he is regarded by the community as a man 'of exemplary life and ardent faith' (p. 56).

This is Silas as we find him at the start of the novel. As it progresses, we see him at three important stages of his life. The first is when he is accused of theft, the second when he loses the gold and finds Eppie, and the last when he regains his gold and is assured of Eppie's loyalty.

When Silas is accused of theft at Lantern Yard, he responds in innocence and trust. He does not suspect William at all, and has complete faith in the lots. He is unable to stand up for himself and lets things run their course, submitting to the dictates of chance. The lots declare Silas guilty, however, and in one blow overturn his life. We see the change at once. Giving vent to his pent-up anger, he accuses William and denounces the 'God of lies' (p. 61). He loses all regard for religion and people; for William, for the preacher and for Sarah. He cannot recognize the fortuitous nature of drawing lots, that they are not directed by God's will, and he feels that the world has betrayed him.

Having suffered such a drastic alteration in his outlook on life, and having 'run away from [his] fellow creaturs' (p. 205), as Dolly describes it, Silas arrives in Raveloe. In this new community he finds only mutual misunderstanding, and he withdraws even further. He is not wholly self-centred, as we see when his jug is broken, but he cannot adapt to village life at all. Neither can he bear to remember his past. He becomes obsessed with the only things he does know: work and money.

All this is the first great upheaval in Silas's life. The change is partly one of character, as his 'trusting simplicity' (p. 57) is betrayed and he loses faith in everything. But the fault lies with Lantern Yard and Raveloe as well; Silas is not entirely to blame. Look closely at the account of the weaver's character in Chapters 1 and 2 and decide for yourself how much he is to be criticized for what happens to him.

The next great change in Silas's life, fifteen years later, begins with the theft of his gold. At first disbelieving, he is then distraught. He cannot communicate with the villagers who now offer help. His thoughts are so much absorbed by the gold that people cannot reach him. Losing the money, however, is in reality beneficial for Silas. It means there is a gap in his world which Eppie can fill. He is at his lowest ebb and so ready to welcome her into his life. From the start, we see the miser's better nature as he finds the baby and immediately starts to care for her, warming and feeding her. He responds to her lovingly, as he has not responded to another human being in years. He decides to adopt and so take responsibility for Eppie, and in the next few chapters we find him learning to look after, educate and raise this new-found, human treasure.

How does Silas change when Eppie arrives? Firstly, he is overwhelmed by love for her, and makes himself her protector. Then, because she is learning all about the world, he has to start taking notice of it too. Because she needs the villagers in order to grow up properly, Silas must also start to mix with them. The people are now very willing to accept him for Eppie's sake, and they are kind to him because of his kindness to her.

Silas learns, through Eppie, to trust God. He goes to church first to have her christened, and then carries on attending the services. As Eppie grows, the weaver becomes more and more grateful to God for sending her to him, and eventually, having talked the matter through with Dolly, can declare that 'There's good i' this world' (p. 205). Because of the happiness Eppie brings him, Silas is even able to start remembering the misery of Lantern Yard and to accept his past instead of cutting himself off from it as he has done before.

At the beginning of Part Two sixteen years later, then, we find Silas a fulfilled man, a man able to trust, to love people and God, and to be accepted by the community. This might seem to be the end of the story, but Silas's trust and love need to be tested. First, he is asked to consider the possibility of Eppie marrying. Silas does not want to lose her, but he also wants what is best for her. With kindness and affection he ponders what to do.

Then Godfrey challenges Silas's right to keep Eppie, and here Silas proves his true goodness of heart. He might fear Eppie is going to leave him, but he does not. He is confident of her ability to make the right decision, and he trusts in God's will. Silas makes no attempt to hide his righteous anger at Godfrey's behaviour, but he also makes no attempt to influence Eppie to stay. This is selfless love, and it is rewarded; Silas wins both Eppie and the gold.

Silas's problems began in Lantern Yard, and he needs to go back there in order to complete the circle. In fact, he discovers nothing there, save that he must continue to trust God and that his real home is now Raveloe. Silas's final words show that he has become a fulfilled person who will love well for the rest of his life, safe with Eppie and her new family: 'I shall trusten till I die' (p. 241).

We are involved in the development of Silas's personality throughout the book; his trials and problems, the way he adapts to a way of life that is alien to him, the way he regains his faith, these things intimately concern us. But Silas also teaches us the lessons George Eliot wants us to learn about life and the way it should be lived.

We first see Silas in Lantern Yard, and the way he behaves and suffers there clearly displays the flaws in this kind of religious persuasion. Notice particularly the way Silas is encouraged to reject his mother's valuable herbal remedies, the natural means of helping other people. He quickly becomes disillusioned with Lantern Yard, but we perceive, if he does not, that his problems there arise from the actions of humanity rather than God. We learn from Silas's reclusiveness that he is mistaken in losing his faith in God and cutting himself off from people.

Like Silas, we also see the faults in Raveloe religion, but we know he is wrong to reject God entirely. When the Raveloe community helps Silas, it is apparent how valuable their way of life and code of conduct can be. Silas is right to go to church in the village and to listen to Dolly's advice on religion. When he eventually learns to trust God again, we know that he is at last in accord with the moral and religious recommendations of the novel.

Turning away from God, Silas fills the void that has opened in his life with an obsessive regard for money, a regard that diminishes him physically as well as spiritually: 'Marner's face and figure shrank and bent themselves into a constant mechanical relation to the objects of his life' (p. 69). It is only when the gold is stolen that Silas can respond to people as he ought. By the time the money is returned, it is comparatively unimportant to him: 'It takes no hold of me now' (p. 226). He has learnt that its place should be secondary to that of human relationships.

It is human relationships that we learn most about through Silas. His withdrawal from people after the affair at Lantern Yard is his greatest mistake. When Eppie leads him back into society, he has found a personal as well as a religious salvation. His kindness to her proves his goodness. He embarks upon a family life to replace the one he lost in North'ard, step by loving step. His raising of Eppie proves him the most exemplary parent in the book, and in the end he gains his reward: his daughter.

By this time Silas has won his place in the Raveloe community. His problems in adapting to village ways have been resolved, and he finds contentment in the company of the Raveloe people. The story of Silas's life demonstrates the most important lesson of the book: that human relationships are the most important thing in life, and that without them we can never be fulfilled.

GODFREY CASS

In Part One of *Silas Marner*, Godfrey is in his early twenties. He has many advantages: he is rich, young, handsome and sure to inherit his father's estate. He has his weaknesses, however. He has fallen into an unfortunate marriage, 'an ugly story of low passion, delusion, and waking from delusion' (p. 80). So that his father will not disown him, and so that he can continue to court the girl he really loves, Godfrey has tried to hide this marriage. He has given in to all Dunsey's demands, lying, cheating and embezzling in order to keep his secret.

When Wildfire's death forces Godfrey into some sort of confession to his father, he is hamstrung by his own indecision (pp. 117–20, end of Chapter 8). In the end he tells half the truth, and this does not solve his problem. Godfrey is still deceiving his father, Nancy and the village, and is still avoiding responsibility for his wife and child.

Even Godfrey's affection for Nancy is to be mistrusted. Instead of coming to grips with the problems that beset him, he pretends that were he married to Nancy, his 'hope of . . . paradise' (p. 81), those problems would disappear. He is being cruel to the woman he loves, leading her on by courting her and telling her he cares when there is no hope of their marrying.

Godfrey sinks to his lowest on the discovery of Molly's body, when with little compunction he earnestly desires her death; 'there was one terror in his mind . . . that the woman might *not* be dead' (p. 171). Then, he refuses to acknowledge his child. As far as Godfrey knows, this means the baby will either go to the workhouse or be cared for by a penniless eccentric whom nobody trusts. In order to protect himself, therefore, Godfrey commits what we know George Eliot sees as the worst kind of sin: wishing harm upon other people. He tries to justify his actions by giving Silas money and promising himself that he will 'be a good fellow in future' (p. 174). He convinces himself that what has happened will be best for the baby and that his behaviour has not therefore been too callous. He seems to have no adequate conception of God or of the heartlessness of his actions. He lives in hope, never admitting responsibility for what he is doing, always believing that something will occur to rescue him from his dilemmas.

At first sight Godfrey's behaviour in Part One is weak and even evil. In fact George Eliot does not condemn him out of hand. She points out that Godfrey is not simply a 'flushed and dull-eyed' country squire (p. 80). He does have emotions. He is genuinely upset and pained by what has happened. He has married Molly partly because of a trap set for him by Dunsey, and now he cannot escape. He knows he is to blame, and he regrets his action.

To confess his marriage would mean the end of everything for Godfrey. He would be as much of an outcast as Silas. His father and Nancy would reject him, he would have no money and he would be ostracized by the village community. We can understand why he is afraid. He turns to Nancy and his affection seems real. He cares enough to do everything he can to marry her, and we see sufficient proof of his love for her later in the book.

A final point in Godfrey's favour is that his family life has hardly helped him. His father has not given him the control and care he needs. He has never been brought up to have a proper sense of right and wrong, so that instead of acting on his own initiative he relies on his luck to sort out his affairs. Perhaps he is not entirely to blame for what he has done.

At the end of Part One Godfrey is hopeful of a happy future with Nancy. At the beginning of Part Two he is forty and his hopes are only partially fulfilled: he wants children and has none. He wants to adopt Eppie, but Nancy will not allow it. He is unable to tell her the truth, and so remains restless and resentful. He is not without good qualities, however. He loves Nancy enough to understand that her decision is not a selfish one and to shrink from hurting her by confessing the truth. He is kind to and concerned about the Lammeter family. He is a good and successful farmer and landlord.

Then, Dunsey's body is discovered. This is Godfrey's moral turning-point. Impressed by the mysterious workings of Providence – 'When God Almighty wills it,' he tells Nancy, 'our secrets are found out' (p. 223) – he summons his strength and tells her the truth. His character has now undergone a substantial change. He really wants to do good. He meets with more forgiveness and love than he had hoped for, and, strengthened by Nancy's acceptance, decides to make amends and right the wrong he has done. Moreover, he sees that his wrongdoing has 'defeated its own end' (p. 224). Had he confessed earlier, he would have had the chance to adopt Eppie far sooner.

Godfrey confronts Silas, and we see in him a blend of motives both good and bad (Chapter 19). He really wants to care for Eppie and to redress the wrong he has done her. He is angry, desperate and humble enough to admit his parentage to her, and he tries to meet her doubts with assurances that Silas will be cared for.

But Godfrey has still not learned his lesson. He thinks he can offer Eppie wealth and status to remedy his previous rejection. He does not recognize that nothing can replace the love Silas and Eppie have for each other; brought up in luxury, he foolishly underestimates the feelings of the poor, and both Silas and Eppie reject him and his way of life.

At first Godfrey is enraged and resentful. His underlying selfishness – desiring to be seen to do what is right, to make a grand gesture and to have his family no matter whom he hurts – has been frustrated. But with Nancy's help he is able to reconsider. He perceives that he cannot buy Eppie's affection, but must 'make her happy in her own way' (p. 236), and that in not being able to adopt the girl he is being punished; he accepts God's judgement: 'I shall pass for childless now against my wish' (p. 236). Finally he turns to Nancy, and for the first time he starts being satisfied with his lot.

Godfrey's character adds a great deal to the book, both in itself and because he shows us more about the Raveloe way of life. The story concerns him almost as much as it does Silas. And, of course, Godfrey's life helps us to understand that of Silas. They parallel each other; Silas adopts Eppie when Godfrey rejects her, and, when the gold is returned to Silas, it is Godfrey who tries to take the weaver's real treasure away. In the end, though Silas is only Eppie's adopted father, she chooses him rather than Godfrey, her real father. Godfrey is bereft, while Silas has everything he desires.

Godfrey also displays mistaken attitudes towards both religion and wealth. At first he has very little idea at all of the former. He puts his faith in 'blessed Chance' (p. 127) rather than in any divine plan. In his early life, certainly, he did great harm without realizing it, and he eventually suffers for this irresponsibility. His marriage is nearly ruined and he never has the family he wants. By the end of the book, however, he has come to appreciate his faults. He admits there is a God, that doing good is important, and that sin will not go unpunished.

As an affluent landowner money is always important to Godfrey, and he is obviously the worse because of this. He judges things in terms of the effective power of wealth. He offers Silas money to look after Eppie, for example, and offers Eppie money in return for her daughterly affection. When, through Eppie, he learns how unimportant riches can be, Godfrey begins to use his wealth more wisely by helping Silas and Eppie without hope of reward.

Finally Godfrey's longing for a family tells us a great deal about the way George Eliot sees family life. Godfrey suffers from his own family, and in recompense he desires a happy family of his own. He does not begin one with Molly because their relationship is based only on physical attraction, without affection or sense of duty. Godfrey hopes for the perfect family with Nancy, and when he is disappointed tries to create one by adopting Eppie. He forgets that true families are founded upon affection, not simply blood ties.

Indeed, Godfrey learns a great deal during the course of the novel. To begin with he is weak and guilty of all sorts of folly. By the end he has told the truth, accepted retribution and tried to make amends. We feel that though not wholly fulfilled, Godfrey has attained a measure of contentment in his life.

NANCY LAMMETER

We first hear of Nancy Lammeter when Godfrey and Dunsey talk about her in Chapter 3. Dunsey mocks her as being too good to be true. Godfrey, however, sees her as the only worthwhile person in his life, the one who will draw him 'safe to the green banks where it was easy to step firmly' (p. 81). Unfortunately it is his attraction to her that makes Godfrey lie and steal, trying to hide his secret marriage and win Nancy back. Though she does not know it, Nancy is the reason for much of Godfrey's wrongdoing.

When we meet Nancy in Chapter 11, we see that she is beautiful, virtuous and a lady, even though she is uneducated and far better at practical housekeeping than book-learning. Everyone compliments her, and she is described as truthful, honourable and refined (p. 148). She obviously loves her sister, and equally obviously has a secret love for Godfrey.

Yet there is something very narrow about Nancy's emotions. She is almost too neat, in her dress as well as in her ideas of right and wrong. She seems too anxious that she and Priscilla should wear identical clothes, and just as inflexible in her decision that having loved Godfrey she will never marry anyone else. She will adhere to this decision whatever the cost, for she is 'exacting' (p. 148) with herself as well as with others. You might like to ask yourself how you feel about Nancy at the end of Part One: are you sympathetic or critical?

By the beginning of Part Two we feel distinctly sympathetic towards Nancy. Firstly it is clear that her love for Godfrey has if anything increased since she married him. She really has done her best to make him happy, thinking always: 'I can do so little – have I done it all well?' (p. 214). It is not her fault that her husband is restless because they have no children, and this is the second reason we now feel more kindly towards Nancy. She, like Godfrey, wants children very much, and her only child has died.

Nancy could in fact have adopted Eppie, but she is determined not to contravene Providence, which seems to have denied her children. Again, this might appear to be narrow-minded; if adoption would make everyone happy, surely Nancy should agree. She holds tenaciously to 'her unalterable little code' (p. 216), however. There is a criticism here of Nancy's religion, which seems set and unyielding. But George Eliot does make it clear that however narrow Nancy's beliefs are, they are genuine. She really believes she is doing the right thing, and that she is putting God's wishes before her own selfish needs.

When Godfrey returns home and tells his wife the truth about his previous marriage and his relationship to Eppie, Nancy's reaction is impressive (p. 224). She forgives him completely and offers to adopt the girl. She also helps him to see how wrongly he has acted. 'I wasn't worth doing wrong for – nothing is in this world' (p. 224). She then supports Godfrey when he confronts Silas and does her best to persuade Eppie to join the Cass family. Here (Chapter 19), as in her forgiveness of Godfrey, Nancy displays great strength of character.

Her desperation for a child is shown by the way she reacts to Eppie. Even so, when the girl makes her choice, Nancy does her best to smooth things over, though she cannot understand Eppie's refusal of the life Godfrey has to offer. Then, without hiding the fact that Eppie despises Godfrey, and without condoning what he has done, Nancy helps her husband to accept his future.

Nancy has an important place alongside Dolly and Eppie as one of the main female characters in the book. She is a complicated person who shows us the problems of a certain type of religious belief, which we can then contrast with Silas's and Dolly's simpler creeds. Nancy also represents one aspect of family life: the good wife who is a childless mother, pining for a complete family. One of her most important roles is to help us understand Godfrey's character, which she helps to shape by being so important to him that he lies and steals for her sake before eventually reforming, again under her influence. She makes him a good wife, and her reward is his recognition both of her value and of the sufficiency of their love for his happiness: 'I got *you*, Nancy, in spite of all' (p. 237).

EPPIE MARNER

We hear of Eppie early on in the book as Godfrey's child, and first encounter her being carried by her mother through the snow to Raveloe. When Molly collapses, the baby toddles into Silas's cottage.

She is a normal, healthy child, intelligent and cheerful. She is mischievous, though seldom really troublesome. She seems to have inherited her mother's beauty, her father's colouring and probably a lively spirit from both. She is a charming baby, and we cannot help but like her as Silas does.

In the first part of the book, Eppie has several functions. She demonstrates Godfrey's character, his weakness and his irresponsibility in trying to deny her existence. Look particularly at the scene where the baby is held in Silas's arms, and, almost in reply to Godfrey's rejection, turns to Silas and begins to 'pull Marner's withered cheek with loving disfiguration' (p. 175).

Eppie saves Silas from himself. She replaces the stolen gold in his heart. Because Silas loves Eppie and cares for her, he starts to see the world through her eyes. Her childish enthusiasm makes him hopeful for the first time in fifteen years. Because of her, he begins to mix with the community, follow local customs, even go to church. Though she is unconscious of the effect she is having, Eppie changes Silas from the miser of Part One to the kindly parent of Part Two.

Eppie and her relationship with Silas show us family life at its best. Though only adopted, Eppie is a real daughter to Silas, and her love is returned. We see how a child should be brought up: with love and protection, not inconsistent punishment. The results speak for themselves.

In Part Two Eppie has grown into a woman. She is almost too perfect, a virtuous fairy-tale princess with long hair and graceful charm. At church, caring for Silas, she flirts gently with Aaron. You might like to ask yourself how you feel about Eppie at this point in the book. Is she a realistic person, or is she too good to be true? Can you find any evidence of her being less than perfect or having any faults?

Eppie is certainly the focus of the second part of the book. Silas's life revolves around her and Godfrey likewise needs her as part of his life. He challenges Silas for her, and it is left to Eppie to choose which father and which way of life she wants.

Eppie's choice demonstrates something about George Eliot's own moral values. She rejects Godfrey to 'cleave to' Silas (p. 234), so teaching both men a lesson; Godfrey is faced with the results of his misdeeds, and Silas now learns that God and Eppie love him and will not betray him.

Eppie here makes the decision to stay a village girl and marry Aaron. She is not tempted by the riches the Casses offer. Her relationship with Aaron is a simple, direct one, based on friendship, common experience and mutual respect. Compare it with the kind of turbulent relationship that Godfrey makes the basis of his marriages.

The conclusion of the book describes Eppie's marriage. She is the centre of attention, displacing even Silas himself. For Eppie and Aaron are now the most important people in the novel, the new generation assuming the reins of responsibility from the old. Eppie will have her own children, look after Silas and found her own family. It is entirely fitting that the closing words of the novel fall to her (p. 244).

DUNS CASS

Dunsey appears only briefly. He threatens Godfrey in Chapter 3, takes Wildfire to the hunt and impales him, and steals Silas's money in Chapter 4. After this he disappears, and the other characters gradually forget about him until the climax of the book, when his body is discovered. Though we only see him in two chapters, however, Dunsey is responsible for a great deal of the action of the book.

He persuades Godfrey to enter into a ruinous marriage, then blackmails him, pushing him to the limits of his endurance, mocking and taunting him and suggesting he murder Molly. Because of his fear of Dunsey, Godfrey embezzles, lies and cheats throughout most of the book. Dunsey then makes off with Silas's money, almost destroying the miser by taking all that is important to him.

Dunsey is the typical blustering country gentleman: drinking, swearing and gambling. He is quick to discern weakness and has no scruples about exploiting it; he twists Godfrey round his little finger and uses Bryce's greed to obtain as much money as he can for the horse. He seems to have no sense of goodness, respect for religion or even any belief in God, relying on good fortune to fend for him – as he says, 'I've got the luck' (p. 79). Like Godfrey he is confidently optimistic about his future, and like Silas he worships money, so that when he falls into the Stone-pits the day after claiming that 'whenever I fall, I'm warranted to fall on my legs' (p. 79), it seems to be a perfect example of divine retribution.

Has Dunsey any good points? His character certainly has little to recommend it, but in the long run his actions are not entirely harmful. It is Dunsey's death that forces Godfrey to tell the truth and make his peace with Nancy. Had Silas kept his gold, moreover, he would never have been able to use the opportunity he is given to help Eppie and to take an interest in people again. Out of Dunsey's actions, therefore, springs salvation for others.

DOLLY WINTHROP

Dolly Winthrop is a product of country life at its best. She is simple, straightforward, kind and caring, with none of the hypocrisy of Lantern Yard or the village gentry. She is 'good looking' (p. 134), conscientious, hard-working and serious. She is a fine wife and mother as well as a good neighbour. On the other hand she is uneducated, often repeating herself in her long, wandering sentences. She is also poor, making lard-cakes with simple ingredients and keeping her children's clothes for hand-me-downs. In spite of her disadvantages, however, or perhaps because of them, George Eliot shows her to be of exemplary goodness.

Dolly's main role in the book is to help Silas. She visits him after the gold is stolen, offering the three things she is sure will help: food, religious advice and the company of her little boy, Aaron. Unfortunately Silas does not appreciate any of these until Eppie appears, but Dolly is not to be discouraged. When the weaver adopts Eppie, Dolly helps him look after the child, though she is careful to let Silas feel his importance to the baby (p. 180). She supports him with advice, practical help such as food and clothes, and tactful guidance over Eppie's misbehaviour.

Dolly particularly counsels Silas over religion. She herself shows us the better side of the village's creed. She is often ignorant and superstitious, unsure of the teachings of the church, yet she trusts God, has a solid, loving family life and is kind to other people. Look at the way she rushes off to help Molly in Chapter 13 and sits up all night with Bessy Fawkes (p. 203).

At first she and Silas misunderstand each other's beliefs. Dolly is disappointed when she cannot persuade the weaver to go to church, but over the matter of Eppie's christening she perseveres: 'you must bring her up like christened folks's children' (p. 181). Silas concurs, attending church with Eppie and gradually learning to appreciate Raveloe religion through Dolly's encouragement and example. Over the years Silas confides in Dolly about his troubles at Lantern Yard. At first horrified, Dolly then thinks things through for herself, unlike so many characters in the book, and comes to the conclusion that Silas should 'ha' gone on trustening' in God (p. 204). With simple but perfect faith and hope, like her charity, Dolly teaches Silas a great lesson, and the weaver owes his new love of life in large part to her.

As well as raising her own son Aaron to be a fine young man, Dolly is of great help to Eppie. She is her godmother, has probably taught her how to keep house for Silas, and is much loved by the girl. It is obvious in Part Two of the book that Eppie has come to rely on Dolly's advice almost as much as she relies on Silas's; concerning her marriage to Aaron, for example.

In many ways, Dolly has acted as a wife to Silas, helping and supporting him. (You might like to compare her with Godfrey's wife Nancy, in her attitudes and views on life.) This is her role in the novel, and it is no coincidence that finally Silas and Dolly go together with Eppie and Aaron to the cottage, as if they were rightfully Eppie's parents.

MOLLY FARREN

Molly is Godfrey's wife and Eppie's mother. She was once an attractive barmaid, but turning to alcohol and opium she became irresponsible and bitter towards her husband. We only meet her once, when in Chapter 12, on her way to challenge Godfrey at the Red House, Molly chooses to drink opium rather than stay awake and care for Eppie. She falls in the snow and dies.

Molly's character is of less importance in the book than the effect she has on other people. Because of Molly, Godfrey is trapped and Dunsey is able to blackmail him; Eppie toddles into Silas's cottage to bring him love; and Godfrey thinks he has to lie for the rest of his life, nearly ruining himself in the process.

Molly is also important as Eppie's mother. She must have given the baby some of her personality, perhaps her gaiety. But she is also a weak, irresponsible mother, refusing to take care of her child and turning her own weakness into bitterness against her husband. Her irresponsibility is comparable to that of Godfrey, who likewise neglects Eppie. Compare her character with what we know of the attitudes of the other parents in the book. What lesson do we learn from Molly?

PRISCILLA LAMMETER

Priscilla, Nancy's sister, is an independent woman: not handsome, but cheerful, practical and kind. She is good at the work she does in running the household. She cares for her father, has raised Nancy and wants the best for her. She is very honest and critical, both about her own faults and lack of beauty and about other people's shortcomings.

Most characters in the book afford us some view of family life. Priscilla shows us what can happen when a woman does not marry and have a family. From the start she is satisfied with the idea that it is possible to have a fulfilled life without a partner: 'Mr Have-your-own-way is the best husband' (p. 149). Sixteen years later, Priscilla is still a confident woman, managing her farm and her father successfully. Although her wistful comment that she wishes she had 'something young to think of' (p. 242) shows the importance of children in everyone's life, we still feel Priscilla is generally content. She is doing what suits her best: 'I shall do credit to a single life, for God A'mighty meant me for it' (p. 150). This is the secret of happiness, which those people in the book who learn to accept God's plan discover. Those who rebel against it, however, do not. Priscilla's life demonstrates this admirably, and she is proof that satisfaction does not depend on having a husband or children.

AARON WINTHROP

Aaron is Dolly's son. As a child, he is talented and bright. He shows us how kind and caring his parents are, and how Silas is so disturbed by the loss of his gold that he is unable to respond even to children. In Part Two, he has grown into a hard-working, responsible member of the Raveloe community. He is the ideal husband for Eppie: a childhood friend who loves her and a representative of the simple village life. When Eppie rejects Godfrey and chooses Silas, she also chooses Aaron, and with him a family life in Raveloe which will be fulfilling for them both.

LANTERN YARD

Although its name suggests light and clarity, the chapel at Lantern Yard is ignorant and benighted. The Evangelical community is made up of poor working-class townsfolk like Silas. They are encouraged to place their faith completely in God, to regard the community as their family and to surrender all self-reliance. Silas is at first very happy with this way of life. Then the theft and the false accusation reveal to him how little trust, support and love the chapel is willing to return.

The three people in Lantern Yard mentioned by name are all sadly lacking in human concern. The church leader, Mr Paston, is a sternly authoritarian figure. He has no understanding of the truth behind the theft and no compassion for Silas's suffering. He keeps to the rules and ignores the complexities of reality. Compare him with the rector at Raveloe, and ask yourself who is the better minister.

Sarah, Silas's betrothed, is a fickle girl. Though Silas does not see it, she is obviously attracted to William, though she does not have the strength of character to admit this. She alternates between being very loving towards Silas and seeming to be repelled by him. We learn that she does not support her fiancé when he is accused of theft, and she finally marries William. We are never quite sure how involved she is in the plan to discredit Silas.

William Dane is the real culprit in Silas's downfall. You might like to compare him with Dunsey: how similar are their characters and how do they each affect Silas's life? William seems worse than Dunsey in some ways, because he conceals his wickedness with a show of goodness. The Lantern Yard community thinks he is saintly, but we know him to be proud and over-sure of his own salvation. He enjoys being the centre of attention, and when Silas's fits begin to attract notice he tries to discredit them, exhorting Silas 'to see that he hid no accursed thing within his soul' (p. 58). William then steals, accuses Silas of the theft, makes off with his fiancée and still manages to make Silas appear guilty while successfully maintaining his own innocence.

William affects the whole of the novel because of course he affects the whole of Silas's life. It is William who destroys Silas's faith in God and other people, who turns him out from the community which was his home and cuts him off from his only family. Because of William, Silas retires embittered and disillusioned to Raveloe, where he becomes a miserly recluse.

At the end of the novel Silas returns to Lantern Yard to find the chapel and the community gone. He never discovers what has happened to the people who nearly destroyed him, but whose malign influence he has at last overcome. As Dolly Winthrop points out: 'You were hard done by that once . . . and it seems as you'll never know the rights of it; but that doesn't hinder there *being* a rights . . . for all it's dark to you and me' (p. 241). The workings of God's justice remain mysterious, and George Eliot makes it clear that, since we cannot understand all that happens to us, a resolute faith is necessary.

THE VILLAGERS

The villagers of Raveloe form an interesting community which at first cannot accept Silas but which finally welcomes him among them. For the first few chapters of the book we are given only a general impression of their lifestyle. They form a tightly knit society: poor, honest and possessing a simple attitude to life based partly on an easy-going religious belief and partly on a real sense of neighbourliness.

It is only when we see the villagers at the Rainbow that we begin to meet them as individuals. There are several characters, distinguished according to their work as farrier, landlord and butcher, and according to their position in the church as parish clerk, deputy and choir leader. Mr Macey, 'our old clerk' (p. 99), is the main spokesman for the villagers and his comments represent what they all feel. He is a pompous old man, but humorous in the way he rambles on, telling the same stories, snapping at Deputy Tookey and giving well-meaning but tactless advice. The stories he tells to the Rainbow crowd about the Lammeters and Mr Cliff are important because they show how suspicious the villagers are of strangers, except those who fit in by being sociable.

John Snell, the landlord, has a natural gift for maintaining the friendly atmosphere of the Rainbow. Bob Lundy the butcher, John's cousin, is a good-humoured, non-committal man. Dowlas the farrier is hot-headed, trying to quarrel with Bob and picking an argument with everyone over whether or not ghosts exist. He and Tookey both have their share of unpopularity in Raveloe. Jem Rodney the mole-catcher is also a poacher; Silas accuses him of stealing the gold in Chapter 7. Ben Winthrop, Dolly's husband, is a good wheelwright, large and jovial. He is leader of the choir, has an important place in the village and seems to be a good and loving father to Aaron. Finally, in Chapter 11, we meet Macey's brother Solomon, who is the region's best fiddler.

These, then, are the villagers. They are vital to the book in many ways; as comic relief, first of all. They provide relaxation between the more serious parts of the book, such as the theft of the gold and the theft's discovery. One has to smile at the petty bickering in the Rainbow scene, the sly comments on the gentry at the Red House ball and the suspicious, exaggerated gossip about the pedlar (pp. 113–15). The villagers help to show us Silas's character and how it develops, furthermore. At first they regard him with mistrust, since he does not conform to village ways. Then, after the theft, Silas goes to the villagers for help, and they judge him more favourably. They do not yet understand him (look at Mr Macey's comments on pp. 131–3), but they do help him. When he adopts Eppie, the villagers really take him to their hearts, and by Part Two of the book Silas's place in the village is secure. At this point the villagers fade into the background as the main drama unfolds, but they reappear when everything is settled. Led by Mr Macey, they give their approval of the wedding – and Silas – with 'a hearty cheer' (p. 243), thereby confirming their acceptance of him.

The villagers, of course, have their faults. They can be unkind, thoughtless and backbiting. Their religion can be materialistic and superstitious. When Silas first comes to Raveloe, their mistrust is terrible; when he helps Sally Oates, they bombard him with their needs and are then offended when he cannot in all honesty help them. George Eliot does not idealize the villagers. They are real people with real faults. Unlike the gentry, however, they are not sternly criticized. Their way of life is essentially a good one. They trust God, and they regard money as useful but not the centre of their lives or something to steal or kill for. They care for other people, have a strong sense of family and of community, and they are proud of their jobs and their place in society. It is a lifestyle of which George Eliot approves, and when Eppie says in Chapter 19, 'I like the working-folks . . . and their ways' (p. 234), she makes the right final judgement on the people of Raveloe.

THE GENTRY

Like the villagers, the gentry in *Silas Marner* play an important part in the book. Few of their characters are well developed, but they act as a background against which the main characters and the story are presented.

We hear some general comments about the village gentry early on in the book, but it is not until the Casses' ball in Chapter 11 that we see them as separate personalities. The Cass family – the Squire and his four sons – are the main landowners in the area. Squire Cass is a typical country gentleman, affluent but seemingly unintelligent, interested only in money and sport. Mr Lammeter, Nancy's father and son of the newcomer to the district talked of by Mr Macey (pp. 99–100), is 'a little hot and hasty' (p. 144), but has raised his motherless daughters well. The Osgoods are an old-established family, related to the Lammeters by marriage; Aunt Osgood talks to Nancy while she is dressing. Dr Kimble is a successful physician, clever and amusing but irritable at cards, much to his wife's annoyance. Mr Crackenthorp the rector joins in merrily at the ball, and is a complete contrast to Mr Paston at Lantern Yard.

These people, like Bryce and Keating, Dunsey's friends whom we encounter briefly in Chapters 4 and 8, are placed apart from the ordinary villagers. This is either because of their profession or because they have land and money. They seem to have enough wealth to entertain, live comfortably and work very little. Certainly the farmers are said to 'farm badly' (p. 54), and all the gentry seem to spend much of their time in one hostelry or another.

George Eliot is less than enthusiastic about the upper classes. They often do not appreciate the value of money, they waste time on idle sports and their 'only work was to ride round their land, getting heavier and heavier in their saddles' (p. 79). They desire war in order to increase their profits, while feeding their hunting dogs good meat (p. 121). There is a discrepancy between the wealth of the gentry and the poverty of the villagers which seems as unjust to us as it must have done to George Eliot. Indeed, some of the gentry appear to regard people as less important than money, possessions or achievement. The Squire, for example, is more concerned about his stolen money being returned than about asking why his sons are thieves. He is a poor example of a father, with little affection for his sons and even less concern.

The gentry do, of course, have their good points. The Squire takes responsibility for his land and tenants and is a fine, jovial host. The rich families in Raveloe may entertain themselves splendidly, but the villagers benefit from the leftovers and 'thought that the rich were entirely in the right of it to lead a jolly life' (p. 71). When Molly is found, the Doctor rushes out to attend to her promptly and efficiently. When Silas loses his gold he is given food, and when he adopts Eppie everyone rallies round to help. In short, the gentry have their part to play in Raveloe society, and they are respected for it.

What is the place of the gentry in the novel? Firstly, they help us to build up a picture of Raveloe life. They provide a background against which Godfrey's story in particular unfolds. By understanding the gentry, we understand Godfrey and Nancy, why they are what they are and why, in the end, they cannot understand Silas's anger and Eppie's refusal. Also, like the villagers, the gentry provide us with some light relief. The Red House ball, like the gathering at the Rainbow, takes our minds off the problems in other chapters.

Finally, the gentry teach us the same lesson that informs the entire novel. Through the gentry, their strengths and their weaknesses, we learn what George Eliot wishes us to learn: that money should not be too important to us, that 'deep affections' (p. 218) do not always accompany wealth, and that real worth depends not on social position but on our capacity for goodness.

Commentary

RELIGION

George Eliot changed her own ideas about religion a great deal in her lifetime. The story she tells in *Silas Marner* has much to teach us about her thoughts on the subject and how it can affect people.

When she was young, George Eliot became deeply involved with the Evangelicalism of her time. The Evangelicals followed a strict code of conduct in their personal lives, and their hopes of salvation relied upon God's will rather than upon their own achievements. They were taught to concentrate on God and on mystical and spiritual things rather than on the world and the people around them.

In her early twenties, however, George Eliot turned away from this extreme creed, losing faith in the religion of her day. For a while she even gave up going to church, although she began to attend again because her family was so upset by her decision. Slowly she developed her own ideas about the right way to live and about the proper place of religion.

George Eliot believed that the way to true goodness lies in caring for other people. Worshipping God is not enough, and is positively harmful when it encourages us to think only of spiritual, other-worldly things rather than the people around us. Religion is also harmful when it saps our self-confidence and makes us rely on the dictates of others without developing our own ideas of right and wrong.

In *Silas Marner* there are two kinds of religion. We see Silas first as a member of the 'narrow religious sect' (p. 56) of Lantern Yard.

This seems to be an Evangelical chapel in a factory town. In the new industrial areas that were springing up in some parts of England at the time George Eliot was writing, the chapels were often the centre of the community. They provided a substitute family life for workers who were sometimes separated from their real families. They provided care for the sick and dying, as when Silas and William look after the senior deacon. They certainly encouraged the workers to live in a God-fearing way, studying the Bible, giving alms to the poor and obeying the Commandments. Silas seems to have led a contented life in the chapel community up to the time the book begins.

There is something very wrong, however, about Lantern Yard and the effect it has on people. Even before the theft, we see that his religion does not allow Silas any self-confidence or independence of thought. He obeys the rules of the church without question. There seems to be far too much emphasis on miracles and the supernatural, such as William's dreams. Anything can be interpreted as a sign from God, even Silas's illness. He is forbidden to consult a doctor and encouraged to think of his fits as visions from above. Instead of concentrating on the people in the community, the members of the Lantern Yard chapel are far too busy obeying their regulations. Under their influence Silas seems unable to react naturally and easily. He even stops practising his mother's herbal cures.

We know there is something wrong in Lantern Yard not only from the effect it has on Silas, but from the other people it attracts The preacher is stern and unsympathetic. Sarah betrays Silas and lies to him. His best friend, William Dane, the leading light in Lantern Yard, is one of the truly evil characters in the novel. He befriends Silas, drains his self-confidence, discredits him, steals his betrothed and isolates him from the community. He does all this behind a hypocritical display of holiness; the other members of the chapel cannot perceive his guilt or Silas's innocence.

It is the theft which really shows both us and Silas the truth of Lantern Yard. When the crisis occurs, he receives suspicion instead of support, and is told to confess and repent. Instead of investigating the matter properly, the community relies on the supernatural authority of drawing lots and is led to the wrong conclusion. Then there is no kindness for Silas in his suffering. Lantern Yard ostracizes him completely. Because his religion has not allowed him to think for himself, he cannot question what has happened. He does not understand that the lots are governed by chance alone, and instead loses his faith in God, other people and himself. While it is obvious that George Eliot condemns Lantern Yard and its effect on Silas, however, she has just as little time for the idol with which he replaces his worship of God: gold.

At first sight the religion he encounters in Raveloe is as prone to error as the religion of Lantern Yard, though for different reasons. Raveloe is conformist, its worship that of the Established Church. The villagers do not go to church regularly, the gentry attending only at festival time and the peasants 'with greater, though still with moderate, frequency' (p. 133). When they do go, the people make the church an excuse to 'eat, drink, and be merry' afterwards (p. 141). The Rector himself is expected to 'set an example in these social duties' (p. 158). People in Raveloe seem very materialistic even about their religion. The church officers squabble over who is more important, and the choir members quarrel about the Christmas money.

The villagers do not seem very certain of the church's teachings, either. There is a great deal of superstition and belief in the supernatural that seems pagan rather than Christian. Dolly seems to think in terms of a plural divinity, and talks about 'Them above' (p. 204). She thinks that Eppie needs to be christened to keep healthy in the same way that she needs to be inoculated. Godfrey and Dunsey base their view of the world on a belief in 'luck' and 'Chance' rather than Providence. The Raveloe regulars discuss the existence of ghosts very seriously and most believe in them. They are just as ready to believe that spirits took Silas's gold as that the pedlar did.

The final objection to Raveloe religion is that it produces people, like Dunsey, who are just as bad as those in the Lantern Yard community. Godfrey has no idea of right and wrong to prevent his lying, cheating and embezzling, or to help him when he finds himself in difficulties. Nancy's 'rigid principles' (p. 216) appear cold and unfeeling. Silas lives in Raveloe for fifteen years and meets only with suspicion, save when he cures Sally Oates and all the villagers run to him greedily for help. It is hardly surprising that at first 'There were no lips in Raveloe from which a word could fall that would stir Silas Marner's benumbed faith to a sense of pain' (p. 64). But when we look more closely at Raveloe, and when Silas and the villagers get to know one another better, we see a different side of their religion and way of life.

Unlike Lantern Yard, Raveloe concerns itself with people, with births, marriages, illnesses and deaths. It is because Silas is not involved in any of this that he is at first not accepted in Raveloe. The villagers do not attend church often, but when they do it is not an occasion of awe but a sociable event that brings them closer to one another. They may be uncertain of their doctrine, but like Nancy they have 'pieced together' (p. 217) a sound philosophy of life that helps them to do God's will, and like Dolly they never fail to help each other out in times of trouble. Raveloe has a moral sense sufficient to recognize and criticize the misdeeds of people like Godfrey and his brother, and in contrast to the Lantern Yard community it can eventually discern and value the true worth of Silas Marner. When he is in trouble, the villagers help. They investigate the theft, aid him with food, pay him social calls and give him advice. When he adopts Eppie, they support him continuously with presents, friendship and 'neighbourly help' (p. 200). This is what true religion is all about.

No one is more helpful than Dolly Winthrop, an ambassador for the village's faith. A good wife and mother, she is always on hand to look after the sick and dying. She gives Silas lard-cakes, baby's clothes and practical guidance. Again in contrast to the people of Lantern Yard, Dolly has thought deeply about her beliefs. They may not be strong on doctrine, but they work. She tells Silas, for example, that she honestly regards going to church as beneficial. It makes her feel 'so set up and comfortable . . . when I've been and heard the prayers' (p. 137). She tells him of her own philosophy: to aid other people and to welcome any good advice. This is very different from the Lantern Yard creed, with its emphasis on spirituality rather than people, and on strict regulation rather than an open mind. Finally, Dolly considers Silas's experiences for herself and comes to the conclusion that 'there's a good and a rights bigger nor what we can know' (p. 204). She advises Silas to trust God whatever happens.

Under Dolly's influence, and with Eppie's help, Silas does begin to regain his faith. He begins to credit the goodness both of other people and of God, who has sent him his child. Because of Dolly's encouragement and because he wants the best for the baby, Silas has Eppie christened and starts to go to church himself. He espouses the religion of Raveloe, though at first it means little to him; becoming part of village life, he becomes happier. He can at last agree with Dolly that 'all as we've got to do is trusten' (p. 204), and when Eppie chooses to stay with him he knows he will retain his trust in God for ever.

Eppie's choice also brings understanding to Godfrey. He learns through the discovery of Dunsey's body that sin will be found out and that evil will be punished. Eppie shows him the importance of love, and, like Silas, Godfrey has learned the meaning and value of goodness by the end of the novel.

At this point Silas wants to take a last look at Lantern Yard. It has disappeared, so he cannot even teach his old friends what he has learned; disappearance, however, emphasizes the fact that Raveloe religion is now the only one that influences him.

Silas Marner changes his attitude to religion as his life progresses, and so do we. George Eliot wants us to see the beneficial nature of the religion practised in Raveloe. It encourages people to care for each other, to rely on themselves and not on the world of dreams and miracles. It makes people better able, in fact, to live in the world around them.

FAMILY LIFE

George Eliot sees family life as the centre of human relationships, and mutually caring relationships as the centre of life itself. She knows that children can change people's lives, bringing them hope and happiness. When she examines family life in *Silas Marner*, however, she criticizes many of the typical families she looks at. The family we are to admire most is very much out of the ordinary: a middle-aged man who has raised his adopted daughter by himself. What then is George Eliot teaching us about family life?

The first lesson seems to be that even when people follow the accepted pattern of family life, things can go badly wrong because people can go badly wrong. At the start of the book, Silas is on the brink of a happy, fulfilling marriage and a settled family future. This is ruined by the fact that Sarah does not really care for him; she betrays him with William and leaves him on his own.

Godfrey marries Molly, but the relationship is based only on 'low passion' (p. 80), not real affection. When disillusionment sets in, the marriage turns sour. Godfrey becomes restless and bitter. Molly hates him for his resentment. Both abandon all responsibility for each other and, worst of all, for their baby. Molly turns to opium, Godfrey turns back to Nancy. He neglects his family until finally he wishes his wife dead and refuses to acknowledge the baby.

The foremost example in the novel of an unsuccessful family is that of Godfrey and Nancy. Godfrey is blinded by his love for Nancy, thinking that after their romantic courtship and ideal marriage he will settle down and 'Nancy would smile on him as he played with the children' (p. 192). Reality is tragically different. Nancy loses her baby, the marriage is childless and Godfrey makes the union even more unhappy with his restlessness. He 'thinks with envy of the father whose return is greeted by young voices' (p. 220). In many ways all this is due to Godfrey's weakness; his unhappiness is punishment for abandoning his original family: 'I wanted to pass for childless once . . . I shall pass for childless now against my wish' (p. 236).

The tragedy of not having children may be difficult for us to understand at a time when large families are discouraged and people actually choose to be childless. In George Eliot's time not only did a child provide 'hope . . . and forward-looking thoughts', as in the Wordsworth quotation that supplies the book's motto, but financial security as well. Children looked after parents in their old age and were also the means of carrying on their name and profession. Dr Kimble is an unhappy figure because he is the last of his family. Nancy therefore worries how Godfrey will cope as he grows older:

'Aged people feel the miss of children' (p. 220). Of course, children are not essential for a happy life. Priscilla, who is sure that God intended her for the single life, seems contented. But even she wishes Nancy had had a child, so that 'I should ha' had something young to think of' (p. 242).

However, even when a couple have children all may still not be well, for the children may turn out badly. This can often be the parents' fault, and perhaps the best example is the Cass family. The Squire is not a good father. He indulges his sons, then turns on them threateningly. He has not given them the discipline they need, yet interferes with their affairs when they fail. So Dunsey is a rogue, Godfrey is weak and indecisive, and the result is an unhappy household 'where the hearth had no smiles' (p. 81).

When people have no love and no responsibility for each other, it transpires, family life is ruined. Does a great deal of love and a willingness to take responsibility then make a happy family? The answer seems to be yes: for example, the Lammeter family is a successful one. Nancy and Priscilla are well brought up and affectionate to each other and to their father. Dolly and Ben raise their children gently though with discipline, and the result is a fit husband for Eppie in Aaron.

The prime example used by George Eliot to show us what an ideal family can be is that of Silas and Eppie. And here, everything seems to be against a normal, happy family life. The two are not related, so there are no blood ties to keep them together. Eppie has been abandoned by her parents. Silas is a middle-aged, single man with hardly any experience of caring for young children, and who has just lost his life's savings. Notice here that Silas's raising of Eppie on his own seems unusual, but that in fact the book is full of one-parent families. Some, like the Squire, Molly and Cliff, fail as parents. Others, like the Lammeters and Silas, succeed. George Eliot is demonstrating that a good family life does not depend on money, marriage or even being related. It depends on the love of the people involved.

Although he might appear to be over-possessive and not strict enough, Silas raises Eppie successfully. In Part One he quickly learns to look after the baby, to dress, bath and feed her: 'I want to do things for it myself' (p. 180). He answers Eppie's questions, makes sure she is always learning and growing, and even changes his own life to improve hers. Look particularly at the coal-hole episode to see how Silas tackles the problem of discipline and solves it through his love for Eppie (pp. 187–8). He himself grows closer and closer to the child, needing 'the touch o' your little fingers' (p. 226), as he tells her later.

In Part Two Eppie has grown into a beautiful and contented young woman; she returns Silas's affection, making them a true family. They see each other's faults and problems clearly, but still care and take responsibility for each other. Eppie looks after Silas and the house and thinks carefully about how marriage to Aaron will affect the weaver. Silas works hard to keep his daughter, and is concerned about how she will fare when he is 'older and helplesser' (p. 210).

The final test of Silas's and Eppie's feeling for each other comes when Godfrey challenges them. George Eliot shows us clearly that ties of affection, built up over a period of years, are far stronger and more valuable than blood ties. Silas loves Eppie 'better than any real fathers in the village seemed to love their daughters' (p. 206). Eppie chooses Silas: 'I can't feel as I've got any father but one' (p. 234). This shows Godfrey how poor a father he has been, and that he cannot expect suddenly to create a family without a lifetime's care and responsibility. Silas's parental love is rewarded, and he will now have a family to care for him in his old age.

The family that will do this for him, Aaron, Eppie and the children they will no doubt have, is George Eliot's final example of the ideal family group. Aaron and Eppie seem to avoid all the problems we have mentioned earlier. They know each other well, recognize each other's faults and will not become disillusioned or let each other down. They willingly take responsibility for each other in a practical way, Aaron wanting to look after not only Eppie but Silas. We are sure they will work together to raise their children well. The book ends with Aaron and Eppie's wedding, but it is a beginning too: the start of a new family that will bring fresh life into the village.

MONEY

Money and its attendant problems were topics George Eliot appreciated. In *Silas Marner* she shows us what happens when money becomes more important than people. Money is part of everyone's life, and most people take it for granted. In *Silas Marner* attitudes vary. In Lantern Yard money is something obtained by work and then either used to buy food, shelter and warmth or given away so that others may do the same; it is 'the symbol of earthly good, and the immediate object of toil' (p. 65). The people in Lantern Yard are, like Silas, encouraged to give their money to help either the chapel or the poor, although Silas and Sarah are saving to get married. So all the money Silas earns has a purpose when he is in North'ard.

In Raveloe food comes from the land and everyone has their own or a rented cottage or house. Money is needed to survive, and the people there use all the money they can lay their hands on. It is not given away, and the villagers laugh at Cliff and his Charity Land. In Raveloe, too, there is a difference between the affluence of some as compared with others. The gentry have land, houses and good food. The peasants have a harder time: they eat cheaply, hand down their clothes and make their children's toys. The difference between them seems unfair but there is very little resentment. The gentry pass on their leftovers to the poor, the villagers come to watch the landowners' celebrations without envy, and, when someone like Silas is in trouble, everyone helps out as they can: 'it was nothing but right a man should be . . . helped by those who could afford it' (p. 200).

In both societies, however, money can cause trouble. When William wants to discredit Silas he does so by stealing the deacon's money and accusing his friend. We suspect that the stolen gold also helps him to marry Sarah. This is the book's first example of the evil passions gold can stimulate in people.

William's action changes Silas's life and his attitude to money. Previously earning, spending and giving his coins away, Silas has taken little notice of them. Once he begins work in Raveloe he has no one he cares enough for to spend his money on, no church to donate it to and more than enough for himself. He devotes his attention to the gold itself rather than the use to which it can be put. It becomes all-important to him. He loves the glitter, the clink and the feel of the coins. He hides his gold away from prying eyes, suspects others of wanting to thieve it and refuses to spend it on anything but his own survival.

Silas becomes a miser, and we see clearly that his elevation of money above people is the worst thing he does in his entire life. He enjoys his money's 'companionship' (p. 68), and thinks of his guineas 'as if they had been unborn children' (p. 70). Yet his love of his gold does not mean he harms anyone else for gain. He earns every penny he saves. Dunsey Cass, on the other hand, will go to any length to finance his drinking, gambling and dissolute behaviour. He cheats, lies and blackmails Godfrey. His life revolves around obtaining money, spending it and then having to obtain more. He is not intelligent enough to consider investment or careful saving, but simply spends until he is forced to commit crime. Finally Dunsey steals Silas's gold, desiring his death in the process, and makes off with it. His punishment shows us clearly the seriousness of what he has done, motivated solely by his need for money.

The theft of the gold nearly destroys Silas. Dunsey's crime removes the focus of the weaver's life. He utters a 'cry of desolation' (p. 93) and views the loss as a 'bereavement' (p. 129); he does not recover from his loss until the arrival of Eppie. The baby takes the place of the money in Silas's life; at first he thinks her curls are the gold, and even when he has adopted her seems 'to see the gold' (p. 226) when he looks at her. And as time passes, and Eppie brings Silas back into the world, she comes to be, like the gold, more and more precious to him. In the end the coins are irrelevant, for 'something had come to replace his hoard which gave a growing purpose to the earnings' (p. 190). The money his work brings is now good money, because it is not merely for him to gloat over. It is to help Eppie live and prosper.

By the time Eppie has grown up Silas has almost forgotten the gold. When it is found again he is glad of it as a safeguard for their future. It has been 'kept till it was wanted for you' (p. 226), he tells Eppie; in those days the poor who had no savings often ended in the workhouse or worse. But the gold no longer means the same to Silas. He now sees it as 'a curse', money 'taken away from me in time' (p. 226). The only thing that could hurt him now would be the loss of Eppie. He realizes that she has saved him from a living death, from burying himself in his money.

At this point Eppie herself has to face the temptation of wealth. It comes from Godfrey and Nancy, gentry who have never been in want, though in Part One Godfrey's troubles were concerned with money. He embezzled from Fowler to pay Dunsey, partly to make sure that he was not cut off from his family without the means of making a living.

Now, years later and secure in his affluence, Godfrey comes to offer Eppie all that money can buy. He reminds Silas that soon he will be unable to work and that his money 'won't go far' (p. 228). Doubting that the poor have strong affections, and thinking that what Eppie and Silas feel for each other is less important than Eppie's material welfare, Godfrey accuses Silas of 'putting yourself in the way of her welfare' (p. 232). Eppie could have fine clothes, a fine house and a good future. Silas understands the implications of what Godfrey is saying, and knows that if Eppie has the chance of such a life he must not prevent her choosing it if she wants to.

Eppie decides against it all, however. Money is welcome, but the love she has for Silas and the good life she has with the working people are more important. Godfrey is mistaken to think gold can compensate Eppie for what she would lose, and wrong to think that the poor and their life are less valuable than what he has to offer. He cannot buy Eppie's affection when he has not won it with a lifetime's love. Godfrey does in fact learn from all this; he must use his money to buy things for Eppie which will ease the life she has chosen, and must help her in the way she wants to be helped.

What are the lessons we learn about money in the book? Firstly, money has its place. It helps us to enjoy life and to live it more fully. But wealth does not necessarily mean goodness or love. The rich do not love more than the poor. In fact, where money becomes more important than affection, either because we want more of it or because we have so much that it blinds us, then we err in the same way that

Silas, Dunsey, Godfrey and William do. Only when we value money in its proper place, as Eppie does and as Silas learns to do, can we hope to be fulfilled and genuinely rich.

CITY LIFE AND COUNTRY LIFE

George Eliot spent most of her childhood in Warwickshire, which in the nineteenth century was a rural area of green fields and villages. She saw a great deal of how country people lived through travelling with her father on his business. She learned to appreciate not only the scenery, fresh air and tiny villages but the rural way of life. She was also a great admirer of Wordsworth, whose work reflected his deep love of the countryside.

At the time George Eliot was growing up, England was changing quickly at the hands of the Industrial Revolution. Industrial areas with factories and mills were springing up in many parts of the country, and life in these noisy, smoky, cramped towns was very different from that of the villages. Many workers who moved from village to town for the sake of employment found it difficult to adapt and felt uprooted and lonely. Factory work was hard and the people unlike those they were used to in their small village communities. Instead of having a common background, knowing and helping everyone, people in these industrial areas had to fight to survive.

George Eliot must have understood these feelings very well, for she herself travelled from the country to the town. Certainly in *Silas Marner* she presents city life as unhappy and country life as rewarding. In the same way she understands the feelings of those who have to exchange surroundings they know in return for those that are foreign to them. Silas in fact moves from the town to the country, but his difficulties in doing so, the way he cannot fit in because he is unused to the new way of life, are those of anyone in new surroundings.

At first we see Silas in North'ard, an industrial region. When he returns at the end of the book, having learned the worth of the country, we are presented with George Eliot's judgement on such towns. Eppie finds North'ard 'a dark ugly place' that 'hides the sky' (p. 239). The streets are narrow, the buildings grim, and it 'smells bad' (p. 240). The people are not well known and friendly but stream by in great crowds, making Eppie and Silas feel unwelcome.

We hear only a little about work in the towns, but it seems to make people unhealthy, 'pale-faced weavers' (p. 58) who were 'pallid undersized men' (p. 51). The work itself is monotonous and repetitive. Silas is said to work 'in' his loom as if merely a handle or cog in the machine rather than someone in control who creates cloth.

Outside work, life in North'ard seems unrewarding too. Like many urban workers Silas has no family. Both his mother and little sister have died, underlining again the unhealthiness of their lives. To replace his family Silas has discovered the chapel community. As explained in the section on religion (pp. 66–70), chapels sprang up in industrial towns providing faith and support for the workers. In Silas's case the chapel is a stern, unfriendly place. The people follow an 'unquestioned doctrine' (p. 63), live a strictly regulated life and are discouraged from independent thought. Silas has to work like a machine during the day, even on Sundays; he is not allowed to think for himself, but must obey. He is even discouraged from the most natural thing he has left, the study of herbal medicines given to him by his mother. He is estranged from everything natural and good; the weavers are trapped 'like young winged things, fluttering forsaken' (p. 58) in the town. When Silas, now betrayed, arrives in Raveloe, he and the villagers are utterly foreign to each other. He has no idea of the Raveloe way of life, for he has never known it. For fifteen years he lives alone, removed from everything.

What is the Raveloe way of life? The village is set in the 'rich central plain' of England (p. 53), in an affluent region deep in the countryside. It is far from anywhere, with a church, a few large houses where the landowners live and a number of tiny cottages for the villagers. We are not given a detailed descripion of the countryside, for George Eliot is more interested in what the people in her book are doing, but we do have a clear picture of an easy, lazy English village.

It seems pleasant, and when Silas later starts to take notice of his surroundings because Eppie does so, we realize how strange and how beautiful the countryside must seem to this weaver who knows only the town.

The country people are described as 'brawny' (p. 51), unlike the pale, unhealthy townsfolk. There are the gentry, the Casses, the Lammeters and the Osgoods, who farm and own land, though not too efficiently; and there are the professional people, the doctor and the parson. The villagers labour and hold jobs necessary to village life: farrier, butcher, landlord. Notice how every person has his or her place in the community, a job that is unique and important, unlike North'ard, where many people do the same sort of dull, repetitive work.

The Raveloe folk all know each other well, and have done so for generations. Many are related. Although this can lead to gossip and friction, it also means that everyone can understand one another's problems and can be supportive, kind and neighbourly. If someone like Silas is really in trouble, everyone helps. This is reflected in their religous practice, which is far more concerned with kindly charity than doctrinal rectitude. The Raveloe way of life is very different to the stern, competitive spirit that reigns in the town, and although at first sight it seems too easy and materialistic to Silas it is in fact a good one, maintaining the village with genuine hospitality, regular celebration and a real sense of community.

Look particularly, when considering Raveloe, at two representative village characters, Dolly Winthrop and Mr Macey; though occasionally ignorant, they are usually well-meaning. Read, too, the scenes in the Rainbow (Chapters 6 and 7) and the Red House (Chapter 11), which show the villagers and the gentry living their day-to-day lives as well as celebrating. They are more human than anything we see in North'ard.

The villagers are not idealized. Mr Macey can be pompous, Dolly uneducated and superstitious. The Rainbow crowd take great delight in bringing each other down, condemning the pedlar and spreading gossip. The gentry can be materialistic, insensitive and even crooked. Even so, as the book continues and, with Silas, we come to know the village better, it is more and more clear that Raveloe life works, and that it is far more valuable than a life in North'ard.

Silas discovers this eventually, and the story of how he discovers it, the problems he has in adapting to the new life he finds and the problems the villagers have in accepting him, form a large part of the novel's interest. At first Silas simply does not understand village ways. When Mr Macey tells him to be 'neighbourly' (p. 132), and Dolly mentions 'church' (p. 137), the words have no meaning. Slowly he learns that, to fit in, one has to learn the customs of a place. When the theft and Eppie have brought him closer to the community, Silas starts going to church, meeting others and learning local ways; he is then accepted. The weaver has not been brought up as a villager and has a very dissimilar background; many of the things he does, therefore, like smoking, he does simply in order to be accepted. They work, though. By the end of the book he has become part of the village and part of the community.

Silas seems to prosper, too. Although Eppie, Dolly and the theft of the gold play the major part in his development, it is set against a background of country life which itself helps in the process. Silas learns to appreciate nature. The easy pace of life draws him into itself. Notice how we see him relaxing in Part Two, rather than working even on Sunday. He is influenced by the villagers' 'open smiling faces and cheerful questioning' and their 'words of interest' (p. 189). Silas is a better person for living where he does, and his final return to North'ard, and his rejection of it – 'It looks comical to *me*, child, now' (p. 240) – show this very clearly.

George Eliot has set *Silas Marner* in country and town for several reasons. In a general sense she intends a criticism of industrialism and the changes it was making to England and to the people it affected. She also demonstrates some of the problems of adapting to new surroundings and how they can be solved. Above all, though, George Eliot is celebrating the country communities she knew so well, and which she valued so highly.

MORAL FABLE

A moral fable is a story which teaches us a lesson about how to live. Almost every society and culture tells such stories, though they vary in form. A moral fable deals with one main character, who has a series of simple adventures. In these he may be threatened, may suffer setbacks for a while, and may undergo trial. In the end good always triumphs over evil. The hero is rescued, often by divine intervention, proves his virtue and defeats his enemies. The story deals with simple ideas of good and bad, and because of this it is often not a realistic but an idealized tale; everything turns out for the best. The lesson is clear; people hearing the story understand what good behaviour is and that it is always rewarded.

In many ways *Silas Marner* is a moral fable. George Eliot shows us what she thinks of as the best way to live, and the novel is a story of good rewarded and evil punished. The main character, Silas, is not a fairy-tale hero, however, but an ordinary weaver, whose story begins when he is betrayed by the villain of the piece, William Dane. Though innocent, Silas meets hostility in everyone around him; even God seems to have turned against him.

At first Silas cannot rise above his suffering, and instead withdraws into miserliness in Raveloe, where more troubles await him. He cannot find a real home. He wanders, like Christian in *Pilgrim's Progress*, and has to face the hostility of the villagers even when he tries to help. Then, when it seems no worse could happen to him, his gold is stolen. We are reminded here both of Christian and of Job in the Bible, struggling under seemingly unbearable burdens.

Parallel to Silas's story is Godfrey's. He too is struggling, but this time the difficulties are his own fault. Godfrey is not a suffering hero in the way that Silas is, but he too faces problems in finding out about himself, in discovering his weaknesses and how to overcome them.

When things seem to be at their worst for Silas, his fortune changes. In a series of 'coincidences' which may be interpreted as divine intervention, Eppie wanders into his cottage, he takes care of her and it seems that his gold has been returned. Silas proves his goodness by taking Eppie in, and he is rewarded, for his love is returned by Eppie and he earns the villagers' approval. His natural goodness allows him to overcome the wrongdoing of others with God's help.

Godfrey's deeds are punished by the loss of Nancy's child and the near failure of his marriage. But he too learns about goodness and accepts that there is a divine plan when, by another seeming coincidence, Dunsey's body is discovered. He finds that he can be rewarded, too: by Nancy's forgiveness and the possibility of adopting Eppie.

Silas also wants Eppie, however; in the struggle for her loyalty, as in all moral fables, goodness triumphs. Silas's love for Eppie is rewarded, Godfrey's misdeeds are punished. The villainous Dunsey has met his death, and Aaron and Eppie marry and find happiness together.

In many ways, then, *Silas Marner* possesses elements of moral fable. One must be careful not to see the novel simplistically, however, as being full of evil villains and golden-haired heroines. It is in fact a very realistic book, set in the early nineteenth century and containing developed characters who are a convincing mixture of ordinary virtues and irritating vices. Furthermore, although in many ways the novel has some of the neatly coincidental facets of fable, such as Silas's opening the door to let Eppie in, it is not altogether idealized. We never know the fate of William and Sarah. They may have done well in life. Neither is the story of Godfrey and Nancy clearly ended. Like Silas and Eppie they will have to return to their everyday lives, to cope with the problems and joys they will encounter in learning to live with the complicated results of what has happened.

Nevertheless, *Silas Marner* is a moral fable in that we can learn from it about God, about religion, about people and about the way we should live. Although we enjoy the book for the sake of its action and the characters it contains, we can also appreciate it for the lessons it sets out to teach us.

Examination Questions

1. 'Silas Marner is an entirely passive character; he never acts, but is always acted upon.' Show to what extent this comment is true. Does it make Silas any the less interesting as a character?

(Joint Matriculation Board, 1974)

2. 'The events in *Silas Marner* express the simple faith that eventually the sinful will be punished and the virtuous rewarded. It is this that makes the story so satisfying.' To what extent do you agree with this account of the novel?

(Joint Matriculation Board, 1974)

3. Either (*a*) 'Hypocrisy is the deadliest sin.' Is this the central theme of the novel?
Or (*b*) The novel should have been called 'Godfrey Cass' not 'Silas Marner'. Do you agree?

(Oxford and Cambridge Schools Examination Board, 1977)

4. Read the following passage, and answer all the questions printed beneath it:

Silas turned a look of keen reproach on him, and said, 'William, for nine years that we have gone in and out together, have you ever known me tell a lie? But God will clear me.'

'Brother,' said William, 'how do I know what you may have done in the secret chambers of your heart, to give Satan an advantage over you?'

Silas was still looking at his friend. Suddenly a deep flush came over his face, and he was about to speak impetuously, when he seemed checked again by some inward shock, that sent the flush back and made him tremble. But at last he spoke feebly, looking at William.

'I remember now – the knife wasn't in my pocket.'

William said, 'I know nothing of what you mean.' The other persons present, however, began to inquire where Silas meant to say that the knife was, but he would give no further explanation: he only said, 'I am sore stricken; I can say nothing. God will clear me.'

On their return to the vestry there was further deliberation. Any resort to legal measures for ascertaining the culprit was contrary to the principles of the Church: prosecution was held by them to be forbidden to Christians, even if it had been a case in which there was no scandal to the community. But they were bound to take other measures for finding out the truth.

(i) Of what crime was Marner accused and what was the evidence against him?

(ii) If there had been a *resort to legal measures* (line 18) what facts, do you think, could have been produced in Marner's defence?

(iii) What method did the community use *for finding out the truth* (line 22)? Why do you think it failed?

(iv) Say briefly how the verdict which was soon to be passed on Marner by the Church changed both his view and manner of life.

(*Oxford Local Examinations, 1979*)

5. Read the following passage, and answer all the questions printed beneath it:

'Father,' she said, in a tone of gentle gravity, which sometimes came like a sadder, slower cadence across her playfulness, 'we shall take the furze bush into the garden; it'll come into the corner, and just against it I'll put snowdrops and crocuses, 'cause Aaron says they won't die out, but'll always get more and more.'

'Ah, child,' said Silas, always ready to talk when he had his pipe in his hand, apparently enjoying the pauses more than the puffs, 'it wouldn't do to leave out the furze bush; and there's nothing prettier, to my thinking, when it's yallow with flowers. But it's just come into my head what we're to do for a fence – mayhap Aaron can help us to a thought; but a fence we must have, else the donkeys and things 'ull come and trample everything down. And fencing's hard to be got at, by what I can make out.'

'O, I'll tell you, daddy,' said Eppie, clasping her hands suddenly, after a minute's thought. 'There's lots o' loose stones about, some of 'em not big, and we might lay 'em atop of one another and make a wall. You and me could carry the smallest, and Aaron 'ud carry the rest – I know he would.'

'Eh, my precious 'un,' said Silas, 'there isn't enough stones to go all round; and as for you carrying, why, wi' your little arms you couldn't carry a stone no bigger than a turnip. You're delicate made, my dear,' he added, with a tender intonation – 'that's what Mrs Winthrop says.'

'O, I'm stronger than you think, daddy,' said Eppie; 'and if there wasn't stones enough to go all round, why they'll go part o' the way, and then it'll be easier to get sticks and things for the rest. See here, round the big pit, what a many stones!'

She skipped forward to the pit, meaning to lift one of the stones and exhibit her strength, but she started back in surprise.

'O, father, just come and look here,' she exclaimed – 'come and see how the water's gone down since yesterday. Why, yesterday the pit was ever so full!'

(i) Why was Eppie anxious to include the *furze bush* (line 3) in the garden?

(ii) Show how the passage reveals the relationship between Marner and Eppie and also conveys an impression of their poverty.

(iii) Explain why *the water's gone down* (line 31) and show how the rest of the story is affected by the fall in the water level.

(*Oxford Local Examinations, 1979*)

Either 6. (*a*) Give an account of the character and part played by

Dunsey Cass, and show how he affected the lives of Godfrey Cass and Silas Marner.

Or (*b*) Write an account of life in Raveloe emphasizing the details which make the village come to life.

(*Oxford Local Examinations, 1979*)

Glossary

Accession: improvement
Addled: rotten
As lief/lieve: rather
Bakehus: house or room for baking
Beau (plural: beaux): admirer, fashionable young man
Beholden: indebted
Bequest: inheritance
Bethink oneself: reflect
Blent: blended
Blowsy: dishevelled, red-faced
Bounden: obligatory
Brownie: kindly goblin which does household work secretly
Carkiss: carcase
Catalepsy: illness with loss of conscious sensation
Chine: backbone joint of an animal
Clave: stuck to
Clew: clue, guide
Collogue: plot
Colly: to blacken and soil
Convention: argument
Demerit: shame
Descry: catch sight of
Dispensation: giving out of laws; the sacrament
Distrain: seize someone's goods to force them to pay a debt
Dubiety: doubt
Eglantine: sweetbriar
Farrier: horse doctor
Fetishism: irrational worship of an object
Filbert: hazelnut
Flekered: dappled, patchy
Fustian: thick, dark cotton cloth
Gallant: flirt
Haft: shaft
Hallow: make holy
Hanker: crave or long for
Inspirit: put life into
Jack: roasting spit
Jigg: dance a jig
Lackered: lacquered
Lethean: making one forget
Lights: lungs of bullocks, pigs, sheep
List: enlist
Mince: be affected, put on airs
Nattiness: dainty tidiness
Nick (road): groove
Noculation: inoculation
Nolo episcopari: 'I do not wish to be made a bishop'; phrase used to appear to want to avoid responsibility
Offal: garbage, refuse
Ort: leftover, scrap
Outwork: the first or outer part of a defence
Perpendicular: erect
Pettish: petulant
Physic: medicine
Pillion: seating for a passenger
Preternatural: beyond what is natural
Rayed: shone
Rended: gave
Rickets: disease which softens the bones

Rutty: rut-filled
Scarify: pain
Seedy: worn
Sensibility: capacity to feel
Sperrit: spirit
Treddle: foot lever on a machine
Twilled: diagonally woven
Vallying: valuing
Vicinage: neighbourhood
Worreted: worried
Yallow: yellow

MORE ABOUT PENGUINS, PELICANS, PEREGRINES AND PUFFINS

PENGUIN PASSNOTES

Carefully tailored to the requirements of the main examination boards (for O-level or CSE exams), Penguin Passnotes are an invaluable companion to your studies.

Covering a wide range of English Literature texts, as well as many other subjects, Penguin Passnotes will include:

ENGLISH LITERATURE

As You Like It
Henry IV, Part I
Julius Caesar
Macbeth
The Merchant of Venice
Romeo and Juliet
Twelfth Night
The Prologue to the Canterbury Tales
Cider With Rosie
Great Expectations
Jane Eyre
A Man For All Seasons
The Mayor of Casterbridge
Pride and Prejudice
Silas Marner
To Kill a Mockingbird
The Woman in White
Wuthering Heights

and OTHER AREAS

Biology
Chemistry
Economics
English Language
French
Geography
Human Biology
Mathematics
Modern Mathematics
Modern World History
Physics

Penguin Examination Bestsellers

Geoffrey Chaucer/The Canterbury Tales

Four English Comedies (Jonson/Volpone, Congreve/The Way of the World, Goldsmith/She Stoops to Conquer, Sheridan/School for Scandal)

Ben Jonson/Three Comedies (Volpone, The Alchemist, Bartholomew Fair)

Arthur Miller/The Crucible

J. B. Priestley/Time and the Conways, I Have Been Here Before, The Inspector Calls, The Linden Tree

Peter Shaffer/The Royal Hunt of the Sun

Bernard Shaw/Pygmalion

Bernard Shaw/Saint Joan

Geoffrey Summerfield (Ed)/Voices III

Arnold Wesker/The Wesker Trilogy (Chicken Soup with Barley, Roots, I'm Talking About Jerusalem)

Oscar Wilde/Plays (Lady Windermere's Fan, A Woman of No Importance, The Importance of Being Earnest, Salome)

Tennessee Williams/Sweet Bird of Youth, The Glass Menagerie, A Streetcar Named Desire

Plus fully annotated editions of your set texts in The New Penguin Shakespeare

Penguin Examination Bestsellers

Jane Austen/Pride and Prejudice

H. E. Bates/Fair Stood the Wind for France

Charlotte Brontë/Jane Eyre

Emily Brontë/Wuthering Heights

Charles Dickens/Great Expectations

Gerald Durrell/My Family and Other Animals

George Eliot/Silas Marner

Oliver Goldsmith/The Vicar of Wakefield

Graham Greene/Brighton Rock

Graham Greene/The Power and the Glory

Thomas Hardy/Far From the Madding Crowd

Thomas Hardy/The Mayor of Casterbridge

L. P. Hartley/The Go-Between

Barry Hines/A Kestrel for a Knave

Geoffrey Household/Rogue Male

Penguin Examination Bestsellers

D. H. Lawrence/The Rainbow

D. H. Lawrence/Sons and Lovers

Laurie Lee/Cider With Rosie

Jack London/The Call of the Wild and Other Stories

Gavin Maxwell/Ring of Bright Water

George Orwell/Animal Farm

George Orwell/Nineteen Eighty-Four

Alan Paton/Cry, the Beloved Country

Jonathan Swift/Gulliver's Travels

Flora Thompson/Lark Rise to Candleford

Mark Twain/Huckleberry Finn

Keith Waterhouse/Billy Liar

Evelyn Waugh/Brideshead Revisited

H. G. Wells/Selected Short Stories

John Wyndham/The Day of the Triffids